The food and cooking of
Belgium

The food and cooking of

Belgium

Traditions ◆ Ingredients ◆ Tastes ◆ Techniques ◆ Over 60 Classic Recipes

Suzanne Vandyck

with photographs by William Lingwood

aquamarine

This edition is published by Aquamarine,
an imprint of Anness Publishing Ltd,
Hermes House, 88–89 Blackfriars Road,
London SE1 8HA
tel. 020 7401 2077; fax 020 7633 9499

www.aquamarinebooks.com
www.annesspublishing.com

If you like the images in this book and would like to
investigate using them for publishing, promotions
or advertising, please visit our website
www.practicalpictures.com for more information.

UK agent: The Manning Partnership Ltd;
tel. 01225 478444; fax 01225 478440;
sales@manning-partnership.co.uk

UK distributor: Grantham Book Services Ltd;
tel. 01476 541080; fax 01476 541061;
orders@gbs.tbs-ltd.co.uk

North American agent/distributor:
National Book Network; tel. 301 459 3366;
fax 301 429 5746; www.nbnbooks.com

Australian agent/distributor: Pan Macmillan Australia;
tel. 1300 135 113; fax 1300 135 103;
customer.service@macmillan.com.au

New Zealand agent/distributor: David Bateman Ltd;
tel. (09) 415 7664; fax (09) 415 8892

Publisher: Joanna Lorenz
Senior Editor: Lucy Doncaster
Text Editors: Jenni Fleetwood
 and Jan Cutler
Designer: Lisa Tai
Jacket Designer: Jonathan Davison
Illustrator: Anthony Duke
Photography: William Lingwood
Food Stylist: Lucy McKelvie
Prop Stylist: Helen Trent
Production Controller: Claire Rae

© Anness Publishing Ltd 2008

A CIP catalogue record for this book is available from
the British Library.

Front cover *Marinated Mussels
(see page 35);* **page 1** *Steamed
Mussels with Celery (see page
57);* **page 2** *Brabant-style
Pheasant (see pages 64–5);*
page 3 *Classic Belgian Chocolate
Truffles (see pages 106–7);*
this page *Onion Soup from
Aalst (see page 27);* **opposite
left** *Toast from Pajottenland
(see page 42);* **opposite middle**
*Breughel's Rice Custard Tart with
Apricots (see pages 118–9);*
opposite right *Blind Finches
with Carrots (see pages 78–9).*

Ethical Trading Policy

At Anness Publishing we believe that business should
be conducted in an ethical and ecologically sustainable
way, with respect for the environment and a proper regard
to the replacement of the natural resources we employ.

As a publisher, we use a lot of wood pulp to make
high-quality paper for printing, and that wood
commonly comes from spruce trees. We are therefore
currently growing more than 750,000 trees in three
Scottish forest plantations: Berrymoss (130 hectares/
320 acres), West Touxhill (125 hectares/305 acres) and
Deveron Forest (75 hectares/185 acres). The forests
we manage contain more than 3.5 times the number
of trees employed each year in making paper for the
books we manufacture.

Because of this ongoing ecological investment
programme, you, as our customer, can have the
pleasure and reassurance of knowing that a tree is
being cultivated on your behalf to naturally replace the
materials used to make the book you are holding.

Our forestry programme is run in accordance with
the UK Woodland Assurance Scheme (UKWAS) and
will be certified by the internationally recognized
Forest Stewardship Council (FSC). The FSC is a
non-government organization dedicated to promoting
responsible management of the world's forests.

Certification ensures forests are managed in an
environmentally sustainable and socially responsible
way. For further information about this scheme, go to
www.annesspublishing.com/trees

Notes

Bracketed terms are intended for American readers.

For all recipes, quantities are given in both metric and
imperial measures and, where appropriate, in standard cups
and spoons. Follow one set of measures, but not a mixture,
because they are not interchangeable.

Standard spoon and cup measures are level. 1 tsp = 5ml,
1 tbsp = 15ml, 1 cup = 250ml/8fl oz.

Australian standard tablespoons are 20ml. Australian readers
should use 3 tsp in place of 1 tbsp for measuring small
quantities of gelatine, flour, salt, etc.

American pints are 16fl oz/2 cups. American readers should
use 20fl oz/2.5 cups in place of 1 pint when measuring liquids.

Electric oven temperatures in this book are for conventional
ovens. When using a fan oven, the temperature will probably
need to be reduced by about 10–20°C/20–40°F. Since ovens vary,
check with your manufacturer's instruction book for guidance.

The nutritional analysis given for each recipe is calculated per
portion (i.e. serving or item), unless otherwise stated. If the
recipe gives a range, such as Serves 4–6, then the nutritional
analysis will be for the smaller portion size, i.e. 6 servings.
Measurements for sodium do not include salt added to taste.

Medium (US large) eggs are used unless otherwise stated
in the text.

Contents

The geography of Belgium

Roughly triangular in shape, Belgium – known as België in Dutch or Flemish and Belgique in French – is located at the crossroads of north-western Europe. It shares borders with France, the Netherlands, Germany and the Grand Duchy of Luxembourg, with access to the North Sea in the north-west. This tiny, densely populated country is blessed with fertile soil and ideal growing conditions. Farmers produce an abundance of fresh foods, ranging from meat and dairy to fruit and vegetables, and, combined with the culinary influences from its neighbouring countries, this has helped to shape the country's superb gastronomy.

Geographical delineations

The terrain of Belgium can be divided into three categories: coastal plains, fertile central areas and the highlands of the Ardennes. Each of these is especially suited to growing and rearing different foods, which has given rise to regional specialties made from ingredients that are available locally.

The coastal plains

Situated along the short North Sea coastline are the two main fishing ports, Zeebrugge and Ostend, which receive daily catches of plaice, sole, herring, cod, grey shrimp, oysters and mussels from the North Atlantic Ocean boats that trawl the waters of the North Sea.

Surrounding these towns are flat coastal plains that are dominated by sand dunes; then, moving inland from the North Sea coast are the polders, a low but fertile land that was once flooded by the sea and rivers but is now protected by dikes.

Central Belgium

Further inland are fertile valleys with clay and sandy soils, irrigated by a number of waterways. The area of Flanders is mostly dedicated to intensive cattle breeding, dairy farming, rearing calves for veal, and pig-keeping. A range of crops also flourish in this region, including oats, rye, wheat, spelt, sugar beets, Belgian endive, hops and flax, as well as potatoes and other vegetables, fruits and ornamental plants.

Hageland, the verdant area surrounding Brussels and Leuven, is called the Green Belt because of its many beautiful natural parks, meadows, gardens and characteristic villages, including the Brussels-Mechelen-Leuven triangle, which is the centre of Belgian endive, asparagus and Brussels sprouts production.

The major fruit-growing areas of Belgium are Henegouwen in the west and Haspengouw in the east, where Jonagold and Boskoop apples and Conference and Comice pears are widely grown.

Below left The beautiful port town of Ostend is famous for its fish markets and restaurants, which make good use of the plentiful daily catch.

Below right Several rivers, including the River Semois, meander through the verdant uplands of the Ardennes, which are prime hunting and hiking territory.

As a result of these fruits' abundance, artisan ciders and speciality fruit syrups, such as *sirop de Liège*, are also produced in these areas.

Between the rivers Vesder and Maas (Meuse) in the province of Liège lies Land van Herve, a region renowned for its historic caves, as well as the production of mushrooms and unpasteurized cheeses that are aged in the humid cave conditions or in cellars.

The Ardennes highlands

Rising from west to east is the higher plateau of Belgium, the Ardennes. This hilly landscape of forests, streams and steep river valleys is home to a wealth of indigenous animals, making it prime hunting and fishing territory. The highest point in Belgium, the Signal of Botrange (694m/2,277ft above sea level) is found here, and is a popular destination for tourists, with ample opportunities for hiking and hunting around and within the valleys of the rivers Maas and Ourthe.

Climate

Belgium's climate is moderate, with regular, gentle rainfall throughout the year. Conditions on the coast are milder and more humid than those found further inland, where the contrast between summer and winter can be more marked. This temperate climate provides ideal conditions for agriculture: a long growing season during which farmers can grow high-quality produce over a long period. Outdoor crops include potatoes, peas, beans, leeks, Belgian endive, cauliflowers, carrots, Brussels sprouts, spinach, cabbages and celeriac. New techniques have also now prolonged the growing period for delicate crops, such as strawberries and tomatoes.

Political and linguistic boundaries

In addition to the three geographical areas, Belgium is divided into three main political regions: Flanders, Wallonia and The Brussels Capital Region. Both Flanders and Wallonia are further subdivided into ten provinces, each of which has its own capital city. Brussels is the federal and regional capital of Belgium, as well as being home to EU and NATO headquarters. Best known as the administrative heart of Europe, it is also a centre of gastronomic excellence, with a range of multicultural restaurants and markets and a concentration of the best chocolate stores in the world.

There are also four main language divisions: the community in Flanders who speak a dialect of Dutch that is called Flemish; the French speakers in Wallonia; a bilingual enclave of people speaking both Flemish and French in the Brussels Capital Region; and a small community of German speakers in eastern Wallonia.

Waterways and railways

The principal rivers in Belgium are the Schelde and the Maas. Located on the Schelde are the picturesque ports of Antwerp and Ghent, famous for its many bridged waterways. These waters are home to several species of relatively rare river fish, such as pike, carp, perch, grayling and barbel, which appear in local dishes. There is also an extensive system of canals, which link towns together and are used by tourist boats to provide a stunning view of towns such as Bruges.

Belgium was the first European country to build a railway system, in 1831. This was used to export vegetable and fruit crops, resulting in the production of these foods becoming a highly competitive sector, ensuring a good supply of top quality ingredients for cooks both within and outside the country.

Above *Bruges is situated on the extensive network of waterways in Belgium. Often called "The Venice of the North," the canals in Bruges were once used for transporting goods, but today they are used exclusively for tourist boats.*

Below *Bordered by four countries and with access to the fecund North Sea, Belgium is perfectly situated for lucrative trading with its neighbours.*

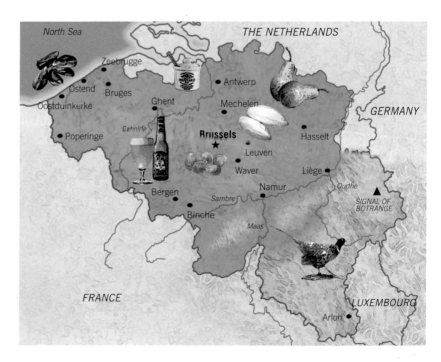

The development of Belgian cooking

The region that comprises present-day Belgium has been invaded and ruled throughout the centuries by various nations and powers, including the Celts, Romans, Vikings, Spanish, Austrians, French, Dutch and Germans. In addition to the cooking techniques and foreign ingredients introduced by these invaders, returning Belgian Crusaders brought with them a wealth of knowledge and foods, in particular spices, from faraway lands. These new flavours and influences were subsequently absorbed and adapted by the local population, resulting in the distinct and highly developed cuisine that exists today.

Early history

During the Neolithic era (5000–2500BC), early tribes lived in small-scale communities, and are known to have farmed cattle, pigs, sheep and goats, as well as growing einkorn wheat (an early, wild form of wheat), millet, barley, lentils, emmer (another early form of wheat) and spelt.

Around 1000BC–AD1, however, the ferocious Celts took over, emerging as a recognizable culture in Gaul (the area that now comprises France, Belgium, Luxembourg and parts of Germany), and imposing their more advanced culture on the indigenous tribes. A powerful nation, these *Belgae* traded freely with Greeks, adopting their coinage and sharing similar polytheistic views.

Despite the prowess of its warriors, Gallia Belgica (Belgian Gaul), as Belgium was called by the Romans, was swiftly conquered by Julius Caesar around 56BC, and became the Roman province of Belgica. The region flourished under the rule of the advanced and civilized Romans, who constructed roads through the forests and marshes, enabling free trade, especially of foodstuffs, and making Belgium one of the great crossroads of Europe. In addition, the application of Roman planting patterns, designed to maximize the potential yield of an area of land, increased both the amount and the variety of foods that could be grown. Indeed, such was the abundance and diversity of the produce that the Greek geographer and historian Strabo (*c.*63BC–AD24) wrote in his work *Geography*: "The Belgae possess great amounts of food, milk and all sorts of meats. Their pigs are allowed to roam free and they are enormous in size and flexibility, for a stranger it is dangerous to approach these animals."

While allowing the Belgae to govern themselves, the Romans introduced a system of local control, whereby each tribe was given a city and an elected representative who, in conjunction with a central Roman civil service in Reims, regulated local authority, building schemes and the maintenance of bridges and other thoroughfares.

Thus Belgium experienced a time of prosperity and, although the natives adopted many Roman customs, some culinary traditions survived. These include the Belgae's method of preserving fruits, such as grapes, plums, apples and pears, by exposing them to the sun or drying them in ovens, the result of which was highly prized on winter banqueting tables.

The Romans also introduced their customs of bathing and spa centres, which centred on the city of Spa, located in the Ardennes. This beautiful town is famous to this day for its mineral waters, and Spa remains Belgium's leading bottled water brand. The sparkling version is sold in a red bottle and the still version in a blue bottle: simply called Spa Rood (red) and Spa Blauw (blue).

The Middle Ages

Following the collapse of the Roman Empire in the 5th century AD, Germanic tribes, and in particular the Franks, whose numbers had been steadily

Below Wheat and other crops have been grown in Belgium since Neolithic times. Today, arable farming remains one of the country's key industries.

increasing in the north and east, came to power and Belgium became part of the Merovingian dynasty under Clovis I. This Frankish King introduced Christianity to the region and started a wave of conversion, which continued to spread when Charlemagne took over in the 9th century and the country became the centre of the Carolingian dynasty.

During this period, Benedictine and Cistercian monasteries became centres of economic and cultural life, and the monks developed model farming methods from which peasants could learn about agriculture. Monks were also great bread bakers, and led the way in developing cereal cultivation. Bread became something of a status symbol at this time, with sifted white flour being used to make loaves for the elite, and rye, which had a greater crop yield, being made into the daily bread for the peasantry.

The monks also developed the tradition of brewing beer, which was used medicinally and as an excellent base for cooking with spices and tenderizing lesser cuts of meats in stews. Milk from the monastery farms was used to produce cheeses, which matured in the vaulted cellars of their abbeys. Today, beer- and cheese-making are still popular traditions in the monasteries throughout the country.

More advanced methods of fish farming were also developed during this period, in order to supply sufficient fish for eating on Christian fasting days when meat was prohibited for religious reasons.

Spices from the East

The Crusades (AD1095–1272) led to a revolution in medieval cooking, and the distinctive cuisine of modern Belgium first started to emerge. The leader of the First Crusade, Godfrey of Bouillon, Duke of Lower Lorraine, and his men brought back spices – nutmeg, cloves, ginger, saffron, cinnamon and peppercorns – from the Holy Land. These were enthusiastically incorporated into local Belgian dishes, including *peperkoek*, a delicious spice cake and *speculaas*, a spice cookie.

Belgium went on to become the centre of the northern European spice trade, with spices increasingly used by royalty and the nobility in cooking and as gifts, or for trading. Condiments such as mustards and vinegars were combined with dried fruits in recipes, giving a sweet-sour flavour to many dishes that are part of Belgian cuisine to this day.

The 12th and 13th centuries were a period of intensive commercial development throughout the southern Low Countries, and cities flourished. Merchants became very prosperous, and powerful guilds erected majestic belfries, guildhalls, and churches that can still be seen in many cities.

For Flanders in particular, this was the beginning of a period of peace and prosperity. The Flanders-Brabant region became highly urbanized, with agriculture as the principal source of wealth. Indeed, such was the diversity and availability of produce on offer that

Above left *This 19th-century painting depicts a romantic view of Saint Clotilde watching over the baptism of her husband King Clovis I, who went on to introduce Christianity to Belgium in the 5th century AD.*

Above right *The Abbaye Notre-Dame d'Orval monastery in the Gaume region is home to a trappist brewery that has been making world-class beer since 1628.*

Great prosperity in industry permeated to all levels of society, with plentiful food for all. The love of the culinary arts is much in evidence in the paintings from the 14th–17th centuries, during which time Belgium became a centre for intellectual, cultural and artistic activity in cities such as Ghent, Antwerp and Brugge.

Among the many great artists of the time are van Eyk (d.1441), Pieter Bruegel the Elder (c.1525–69), his son Jan Brueghel the Elder (1568–1625), Rubens (1577–1640) and van Dyck (1599–1641). These artists often portrayed scenes of food and feasting, and one of the most notable of these is Pieter Bruegel the Elder's painting *The Battle between Carnival and Lent* (1559), which depicts a woman carrying honeycomb cakes with indentations, which were baked in flat irons. These were called *wafla* or *wafel* in old Frankish, and were sold warm to the people on the street. Still a favourite snack today, waffles represent the continuation of traditions and remain a major part of modern Belgian cuisine.

Above This close-up detail of a section of the painting The Battle between Carnival and Lent *by Pieter Bruegel the Elder shows a woman carrying a table bearing bread rolls and waffles, revealing the existence of* wafla *or* wafel *in Belgium as long ago as 1559.*

the Flemish physician and botanist Rembert Dodoens wrote a directory of the herbs, plants and vegetables in his *Cruydenboeck* (1583) – considered one of the foremost botanical works of the late 16th century.

A Golden Age

When the Low Countries became part of Burgundy (c.1369), wine from the region was introduced to the Belgian upper classes, who held sumptuous banquets as a major part of the celebrations for ducal weddings and meetings of the chivalric Order of the Golden Fleece, and this affinity with Bordeaux and Burgundy wines remains strong today.

Foods from further afield

As time moved on, ingredients such as tomatoes, sugar cane, rice, potatoes, coffee and cacao arrived from the newly discovered Americas. Their use, in combination with the ingredients from other cultures, meant that the 16th-century Belgian kitchen was more advanced than those of neighbouring France and Germany. Evidence of this can be seen in Lancelot de Casteau's cookbook, *Ouverture de Cuisine* (1604), which contains the first potato recipe.

Right This oil painting by Jan Brueghel the Elder, The Sense of Taste, *from 1618 depicts the Belgians' love of fine foods and lavish feasting in the 17th century.*

Foreign domination of Belgium

After the Burgundian rule there was a period of foreign domination by Spain that lasted until Napoleon Bonaparte came to power and Belgium became part of the French empire at the beginning of the 19th century. During this period, Belgian cooks adopted and adapted cooking styles from the French, integrating them as part of their culinary repertoire. This is evident in the work of the forefather of French-Flemish gastronomy, Philippe Cauderlier from Ghent, who published a cookbook in 1861 called *l'Economie Culinaire*. In it he described classic Flemish dishes that had been modified to include traditional French techniques. One of these is *beefsteack met aerdappelen*, a primitive version of the national dish *steak frites*.

Following the defeat of Napoleon at Waterloo in 1815, Belgium was ceded to the newly formed kingdom of The Netherlands. Catholic, French-speaking Belgians fiercely resisted the imposition of the Dutch and Flemish languages and Protestant religion and, in 1830, Belgium declared its independence from The Netherlands, adopted a constitution, and chose its first king: Leopold I.

This was also the year that Belgian endives were said to have been discovered by accident by a farmer called Jan Lammers. Having put some chicory into storage in a cellar while he went to war, he found upon returning that they had sprouted distinctive white leaves. It then took around 40 years of refinement by Mr Bezier, head of the Brussels Botanical Gardens, for the vegetable to be suitable for commercial growth but, in 1872, it was finally introduced in Paris, where it was so popular and in such demand that it was dubbed "white gold".

Towards modern Belgium

The neutrality that had been granted to Belgium following its independence in 1830 lasted until the country was occupied by the Germans during World War I and World War II (1914–18 and 1939–45). During this time the local population suffered much hardship, with food becoming scarce and people existing on a meagre diet of potatoes, herrings and porridge.

To meet the demand for coal workers in an increasingly industrialized nation after World War II, many immigrants came to Belgium from Italy, Turkey and North Africa. These people brought their cuisines with them – and today Italian cuisine is the second favourite type of food in Belgium.

Present-day Belgium is a federal state with one of the most open economies in the world. Its stance on trade is attributed to its historical reputation in international business, with the capital city Brussels as its cosmopolitan hub. As a result of this open international outlook the capital is bursting with new and innovative global cuisines, which are enjoyed by Belgians and visitors alike.

Despite the presence of international cuisines throughout the country, however, classic Belgian food is still extremely popular, and the nation's devotion to its culinary traditions remains strong. In this spirit of taking pride in their cuisine and enjoying food, Belgians bring a certain *joie de vivre* to the family table, where the importance of friends, family and a good meal prevails.

Left The Botanical Gardens in Brussels was the site of more than 40 years' research and refinement by Mr Bezier, who eventually produced Belgian endives that were suitable for commercial growth.

Below Belgians are fiercely proud of their cuisine and, despite the increasing number of foreign restaurants. Most people enjoy visiting a traditional eaterie serving much-loved classic dishes.

Regional dishes and specialities

The common characteristics that unite the ten provinces in Belgium are the national love of breads in all their forms and an abundance of sweet and savoury baked pastries, and chocolates and candies. Aside from these ubiquitous foods, the origins of many of Belgium's dishes can be traced to individual villages or provinces, such as the Matten tartlets, which are made only in and around the area of Geraardsbergen. Because of the different historic influences and the various dialects spoken in these locations, regional foods often have whimsical nicknames or contain an unusual ingredient.

Fish and shellfish

Although most of the salt water fishing takes place out in the North Sea, an ancient method of shoreline fishing is used in Oostduinkerke. Here, fishermen drag their nets close to the shore at low tide behind their legendary Brabant draft horses, scooping up grey shrimp. These are then sold to the coastal restaurants in Flanders to be cooked in the classic dish of tomatoes filled with shrimps, *tomate crevette*.

Freshwater fish from rivers and streams appear in various local dishes, such as eel in green chervil sauce – a speciality of both East and West Flanders, and *truite à l'Ardennaise* (Ardennes-style trout). In Brussels, the ancient tradition of eating *caracollen*, tiny sea snails in court bouillon, continues, and the snails are sold as street food at fairs and markets.

Right *The fishermen of Oostduinkerke are famous for dragging nets for grey shrimp along the shoreline on horseback.*

Below *Smoky, flavoursome Ardennes ham is a much-loved regional speciality in south Belgium.*

Poultry, meat and game

Chicken is a favourite ingredient all over the country although Brussels still bears its nickname *kiekefretters* ("chicken eater") due to its inhabitants' love of a range of dishes made with the meat. There is a range of breeds available to buy, but the Coucou de Maline, a speciality breed from Mechelen, is considered the best.

East Flanders and the Ardennes are renowned for their smoked hams, *jambon d'Ardennes* and *vlaamse been hesp* or *ganda* ham. Flanders' pastures provide pigs that produce a ham that is more tender and milder in flavour than the ham from the Ardennes, which has a smoky taste and a dry texture. These differences are due to the feed the pigs are given, as well as the method of hanging the hams over smoking juniper wood that is used in the Ardennes.

Certain areas in Belgium are notable for horsemeat, a tradition that harks back to the eating habits of the Celts. The city of Vilvoorde (Brabant) is most famous for its horse markets, where "horse steak" is cooked in horse fat and served with *frites* and mayonnaise. *Schep*, a horse stew from the area of Willebroek (Antwerp), is served at special festivities.

Vegetables

Belgian endives and white asparagus are especially popular in Kampenhout (Brabant), where specialist restaurants offer menus featuring these star ingredients. Dishes range from soups and appetizers to main dishes, with *endive au gratin* and *asperges à la Flamande* being among the top choices.

Deriving their name from the region in which they were first cultivated, Brussels sprouts are now enjoyed all over Belgium. Another speciality from the Brussels region, *stoemp* (mashed potato mixed with other vegetables) is often served with blood sausage and a local beer, and makes a frequent appearance on cold winter days.

Tender, delicate hop shoots (sometimes called "hop asparagus") may be served as part of either hot or cold dishes, and are one of the priciest vegetables on earth. Cultivated only in the areas of Poperinge and Asse, they make a star appearance for just four weeks between March and April.

Fruits

The Haspengouw region is a fruit-growing area *par excellence* that produces many fresh fruits and fruit products, including apple ciders and *sirop de Liège* – a sweet, thick syrup made from cooked-down pears, apples and dates, which can be spread on pancakes or breads or added to sauces to accompany game or meat. Today, sadly, only a few enterprises making such regional syrups are left, so it can be hard to find.

Dairy

Every city has a speciality cheese store (*fromagerie/ kaaswinkel*), offering hundreds of different regional varieties, ranging from fresh white cheeses to mild or strong, matured cheeses. In addition to Brussels *hettekees* and the ancient-style Herve cheeses, others are often named after specific regions or castles, such as Wynendale, or abbeys such as Chimay, Maredsous, Westmalle, Orval, Corsendonk and Postel.

Bread and pastries

In addition to the two types of *pistolets* (crunchy round bread rolls and soft, slightly sweet, oval-shaped rolls called *sandwich*) that are found throughout the country, each region in Belgium has its own speciality bread. These include *cracquelin* from Liège (a soft white bread made with pearl sugar, eggs and butter) and *mastellen* (cinnamon rolls) from Ghent.

A key feature of Belgian's gastronomy is its pastries and its reverence for the fine-quality pastry shops (*patisseries*) that are present all over the country. Local delicacies such as *speculaas* (spice cookies) are sold nationwide, although there are some regional twists on the classic recipe. These include the famous *speculaas* from Hasselt, the recipe for which is linked to local *genever* production as it uses the burnt sugar left over from the process of making the drink.

As well as the spices used in *speculaas*, almonds are a key ingredient in many pastries, including the delectable almond tart from Diksmuide. Savoury pastries, such as the ancient *tarte al djote* from Nivelles (made with pungent fermented cheese and chard or beet leaves) are also much enjoyed.

Mustard

Ghent is home to one of the oldest mustard manufacturers, Tierenteyn, which has been in operation since 1790. In addition to this company, a small number of artisan mustard manufacturers still remain throughout the country.

Sweets

Brussels is the birthplace of the praline, a luxury chocolate-filled sweet that was introduced by Jean Neuhaus Jr in 1912. A true Belgian speciality, it is found in more than 2,000 chocolate stores all over the country. Stylishly packaged *ballotins* include round or square pralines filled with liqueur and a variety of chocolate flavours. There are also numerous candies and cookies with amusing names, such as *babbelaars* or *babelutten* ("someone who talks a lot"), a caramel-like candy made in Ieper and Veurne (West Flanders).

Drinks

Belgium is world famous for its beers. Among the countless regional varieties there are a few that stand out, including Gueuze and Lambic. Brewed only to the west of Brussels, the most significant characteristic of Lambic is that it is allowed to ferment spontaneously by being exposed to the unique microflora from the Senne Valley, called *Brettanomyces bruxellensis*. It is then fermented for a second time in oak barrels, which lends it a sweet-sour taste, infused with sour cherries.

Other beers include the legendary rich, dark Trappist varieties, including Chimay, Orval, Rochefort, Westmalle, Westvleteren and Achel, and abbey beers, such as Leffe, Duvel, Corsendonk, Kwak, Karmeliet and Affligem. These beers were originally produced by monks as part of their ancestral tradition of brewing. Each should be drunk from a specific glass, the shape of which is said to enhance the beer's characteristics.

Several medieval brewed liqueurs are still produced. These include Elixir d'Anvers (Antwerp), a herbal liqueur for nightcaps and medicine, and Elixir de Spa, a drink composed of over 40 plants and herbs.

Top *Artisan mustards, such as these ones made by Tierenteyn, are sold in specialist condiment shops.*

Middle *Speciality cheese stores stock a wide range of regional cheeses, such as this one from Bruges.*

Above *The popular* sirop de Liège *is one of the few regional fruit syrups still made in Belgium.*

Belgian eating habits

From a culinary standpoint, Belgium has always been unfairly placed in the shadow of its French neighbour and it is a little known fact that Belgium has more Michelin-starred restaurants per capita than France. Belgians enjoy their culinary heritage, and if a person has a reputation for enjoying good food, drink and life in general they will refer to themselves as "Burgundiers" or with a "Burgundian lifestyle". This reference alludes to the Burgundian era when art and food were especially celebrated in Belgium, and is a philosophy of fine dining that is very much alive among every generation, including the young.

Family life
The family plays a vital role in Belgian society. Since most people continue to live in their hometown upon reaching adulthood, weekends are usually dedicated to visiting family members for lunches or dinners to catch up on the past week's events.

Breakfast
For most Belgians, breakfast usually starts with a *boterham* or *tartine*: two slices of white or wholegrain bread spread with *chocopasta* (chocolate paste), or filled with a slice of *speculaas* (spice cookie) or *peperkoek* (spice cake). Also on offer are an assortment of cold cuts (charcuterie), cheeses and jams, accompanied by coffee, tea or milk. During the weekends and holidays the breakfast table extends itself to a variety of breads, *pistolets* (bread rolls), sugar, raisin and chocolate breads and *koffiekoeken* (breakfast pastries). Belgians enjoy taking time for their meals, and a Sunday breakfast can last at least an hour.

Right Soup, such as this one made with watercress, is often served for lunch, followed by a potato dish accompanied by meat or vegetables.

Below Assorted breads, including soft white loaves and rustic granary versions are sold in bakeries and eaten with every meal.

Lunch
The midday meal will begin between 12 p.m. and 1 p.m. and traditionally consists of soup, followed by potato, vegetable and meat dishes and a dessert or some fruit. However, because of modern working patterns, weekday lunches are more often a sandwich taken to work or school and perhaps combined with soup or a salad. Bottled sparkling or spring water and a range of other drinks are usually served with lunch.

Snacks and street food
Afternoon snacks play an important role in a Belgian's daily life, as they love to socialize around a small bite to eat. In the afternoon many people take a coffee break and enjoy a pastry, pie, waffle or pancake with friends and colleagues in a coffee salon or patisserie. On sunny days, terraces of brasseries fill up with people buying a refreshing Dame Blanche ice cream (ice cream with a chocolate sauce), or indulging in a

toast cannibale (toast with a raw meat topping) or *croque monsieur* (a grilled ham and cheese sandwich). These are accompanied by a cold drink. Waffles, ice creams and *frites* are also sold everywhere on the streets for those in a hurry, and a *frietkot* (*fritos* booth) or warm waffle stand will never be too far away.

Supper

Between 6 and 7 p.m., depending on the quantity eaten for lunch, a warm three-course menu will be prepared, traditionally starting with soup and followed by a meat, potato and vegetable platter, and dessert – mostly enjoyed with wine or beer. If a hot lunch was eaten, however, a simple meal with bread, cheese and cold meats will suffice. Consequently, bread is eaten at least twice a day, a habit that suits the bread-loving Belgians.

Socializing, eating out and restaurant parties

Going out for dinner to a restaurant is a social event, and a table will usually be booked for the entire night. Dining is still the preferred way of meeting friends and family, allowing hours of quality time over good food and drink. Diners usually start with an aperitif, which can vary from cocktails to beers and wine, accompanied with appetizers or *amuse bouches* (tiny morsels to eat), which allow the diners time to decide upon a selection of first courses, side dishes and desserts. Although beer is widely consumed, good-quality French wines are still the drink of choice for elegant entertaining.

The entire menu selection is most often dictated by the seasons. During the winter months, hearty dishes such as stews, game and winter vegetables (such as *endive au gratin*) will be offered, whereas a spring and summer menu will feature the assorted delights of fresh vegetables and fruits or seasonal fish, including the many glorious mussel dishes.

For those who prefer not to spend their entire night in a restaurant, "going for a drink" to a local cafe or tavern at around 9 p.m. is a popular weekend activity. Here people meet friends and enjoy a drink and a small bite to eat. Later at night, many will head for a cone of *frites* or small snack to satisfy late-night hunger pangs.

Socializing at home with intimate dinners for friends and family is also very common. Cheese and wine evenings, where a tray of various breads and cheeses is offered with complementary wines or beers, are popular entertaining events. Bringing a *ballotin* of pralines as a gift for the host is the most common gesture when invited to someone's home.

Etiquette

Belgians take great pride in their appearance, their cuisine and the impression they give to others, and this is reflected in their eating styles and decorous table manners. Good table etiquette is expected when dining out, and using the right cutlery with each course and the correct glass with the appropriate drink is of utmost importance for an enjoyable meal.

Above Friends and families enjoy socializing over a meal consisting of their favourite foods, such as mussels or steak served with frites *and beer.*

Left Frites are a favourite food and can be eaten as an accompaniment to other dishes, or on their own as a snack, served in a paper cone or tray, often with a dollop of mayonnaise.

Festivals and celebrations

Belgians are an intriguing combination of Gallic and Germanic cultures and there are many political differences between the regions. Despite this, the people have a strong national identity and a determination to protect and preserve their history, a fact that is evident in the many regional festivities celebrating ancient pagan and religious events that still take place in every part of Belgium. For hundreds of years these festivals have involved lavish food events with many speciality foods on offer, such as *smoutebollen*, *pepernoten*, *moppen*, *nic-nacs*, *speculaas* and other delectable items.

Village fairs

Kermis is an annual village festival tradition that dates back to the 16th century, when it originated as a religious event to commemorate the patron saint of the city or village. The celebrations included a procession and a *kermis* (fair) that lasted eight days. Although the processions have mostly disappeared, the *kermis* is very much alive. This excitedly awaited event features food stalls selling typical fair produce: *frites*, sausages, shrimp croquettes, *smoutebollen* (fritters dusted with powdered sugar), apple beignets, light and airy waffles from Brussels, or sugary and dense ones from Liège – and much more.

Pilgrimages, processions and carnivals

Christian devotion and pageantry is very much alive all over Belgium and there are numerous events during the year. These include a candlelit procession for Our Lady of Scherpenheuvel, which dates back to the Spanish occupation of the 16th century. This takes place in the small town of Scherpenheuvel on the Sunday after All Saints' Day. However, because thousands of pilgrims visit the town throughout the year, there is always a celebratory atmosphere, with stalls selling souvenirs and typical sweets like the *pepernoten* and *moppen*.

The Procession of the Holy Blood is another important event, and it has taken place in Bruges each May since 1303. During the religious pageant, the relic of the Holy Blood is carried at the head of a mile-long procession of more than 1,500 Bruges citizens, who dress up in medieval garb.

One of the most famous festivals is the Binche festival, which has been classified by UNESCO as part of the world's cultural heritage. Dating from 1549, the three-day carnival take place in February. During the festivities, men called *gilles* dress in bright costumes and some wear high, plumed hats. Having eaten a breakfast of oysters and champagne at 4 a.m., they then take part in parades, letting off fireworks and throwing small blood oranges into the crowd on the Grand Place, while spectators feast on local double-buckwheat pancakes filled with Herve cheese, called *les doubles de Binche*.

Below left Waffles, such as these ones from Liège, are among the many delectable treats on sale at food stalls at a kermis.

Below right Children cut off the head of the lamb-shaped cake made from ice cream that is served at their first communion.

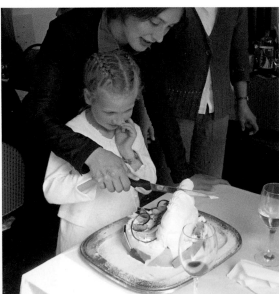

Saint Nicholas

The legendary bishop Sinterklaas, or Saint Nicholas (AD270–343) is the patron saint of Belgian children and makes his entrance every year on 6 December. He brings presents and sweets, including moulded hollow chocolate and figures made from sculpted marzipan, *nic-nacs* (tiny biscuits dusted with icing (confectioners') sugar), *guimauve* (soft candy shaped in the form of St Nicholas or Mother Mary), gold-wrapped chocolate coins, and mandarins.

In addition, spice cookies, *speculoos*, or *speculaas*, are eaten for this celebration. The name derives from the Latin *specula*, meaning mirror, because the cookies were originally pressed into wooden moulds of various designs showing pictures of people or animals. In medieval times doll-shaped *speculaas* were given by men to girls as a way of proposing.

Christmas, New Year, Three Kings' Day

Families share special meals at home during Christmas. They will start with aperitifs followed by an appetizer, which may be fish or shellfish, and then the main course, which is often game, goose, duck, turkey or roast lamb accompanied by a variety of vegetables and a potato dish (such as potato croquettes). For dessert many choose a *bûche de Noël* (Christmas log). For New Year the ritual is similar, although it is often celebrated with friends in restaurants and combined with dancing parties.

For Three Kings' Day (Epiphany) on 6 January, children dress up in costumes and go from door to door singing and receiving money and candy. This custom dates back to the 19th century, when the peasants were given waffles and cookies by the rich,

and bread by the monks at the local monastery. In recognition of this, rich foods such as pancakes, waffles, crown-shaped king cakes, apple dumplings and sausage breads are enjoyed.

Easter

On Easter morning children participate excitedly in Easter egg hunts. The story goes that the church bells leave for Rome on the Saturday, returning on the Sunday with chocolate eggs, which they drop into the children's gardens. The Easter bunny then helps to hide them for the children to find.

According to traditional religious beliefs no animal products can be consumed up to 40 days before Easter, so Easter itself is a time for the celebration of food. Breakfast will start with soft sugar breads, often enclosing boiled eggs, and lunch and dinner usually consist of poultry or lamb and egg dishes, such as *vogel nestjes* (bird's nests). The consumption of eggs symbolizes the victory of light over the long dark winter and the beginning of the fertile period of spring.

Births, christenings and weddings

Other events during the year are also celebrated with food. Friends and families visiting a newborn baby are welcomed with *suikerbonen* – small decorated packages of pastel-coloured, sugar-coated pastilles filled with almond paste or chocolate. Weddings and christenings are celebrated by throwing elaborate parties with multiple and varied buffet menus.

For a child's first communion an *ijslam* is made. This is a cake in the shape of a lamb formed out of ice cream. The child traditionally cuts off the lamb's head so that a grenadine syrup or raspberry coulis that is inside drips on to the ice cream.

Above On Easter morning children hunt for chocolate eggs, said to have been brought from Rome by the church bells and hidden by the Easter bunny.

Left Wooden *speculaas* moulds are often used to make the traditional spice cookies that are served at Sinterklaas.

Classic Belgian ingredients

Belgium's cuisine was heavily influenced by events in the Middle Ages, a fact that is reflected in its use of condiments, mustards and spices to enhance simple dishes. Throughout the ages the country's cooks have remained loyal to traditional kitchen practices, while being willing to accept new ideas if they enhanced their own food. This devotion to national favourites was noted in the first edition of the *Larousse Gastronomique* in 1938, which states: "Les Belges, fin gourmands, étaient restés jalousement fidèles à leurs vieux plats nationaux" ("Belgians, fine gourmands, stayed jealously loyal to their national dishes").

Seafood

Belgians are passionate about shellfish, with North Sea molluscs making up a large proportion of the nation's annual consumption of shellfish, oysters, sea snails, scallops and, of course, mussels. *Moules* are the national dish and are prepared in numerous creative ways. The mussels are usually served in a special steaming pot, the lid of which serves as a dish for the empty shells, and are extracted with a discarded shell, which is used to pull out each succulent sea creature. Each portion is accompanied by a portion of *frites* and mayonnaise on the side.

In addition to shellfish, a variety of fish species are brought in by Belgian fishing boats to the harbours of Ostend and Nieuwpoort. These include cod, sole, herring, turbot and monkfish as well as freshwater stream and river fish, such as trout and eel.

Meat, poultry and game

Although there is extensive beef farming in the area of West Flanders, Namur and Liège, pork is the favourite meat. Numerous pork dishes can be found on the menu – from pork chops, sausages, terrines, hams and the traditional pressed meat made with pig's cheeks called *kip kap*, to *potjesvlees*, a specialty from in and around Veurne (made with a mixture of chicken, veal and rabbit), served with mustard and beer. Belgium's other national dish, *steak frites*, and the medieval *carbonnades à la Flamande* indicate that over the years beef has become popular. Veal is also one of the top choices, savoured in dishes such as *blanquette de veau* (veal ragout in white cream sauce).

Poultry and game have been eaten in Belgium since the early Middle Ages, and appear in numerous dishes, such as roast chicken with apple sauce or Ghent-style chicken stew. A wide variety of game is hunted during the season in the forest region of the Ardennes, including pheasant, partridge, capon, venison, wild boar, stag and roebuck, and classic as well as newly created game dishes are plentiful on the autumn menus there. Rabbit and hare dishes are often prepared with the addition of speciality beers and combinations of fruits and spices, which complement the succulent meat perfectly.

Dairy

In spite of the fact that Belgium is such a small country, it produces more than 300 distinct varieties of artisan cheeses and milk product derivations, which are mostly consumed by the Belgians themselves rather than being exported. The cheeses are enjoyed with Belgium's exquisite country breads and renowned beers.

Vegetables

Few other countries have developed and perfected as many vegetables as Belgium, including Belgian endives, white asparagus, Brussels sprouts, salsify, celeriac, kohlrabi, hop shoots, potatoes, mushrooms and much more, all of which are abundant due to the humid climate, fertile soil and skilled horticulturists.

Witloof (chicory or Belgian endives) is a unique Belgian vegetable with white, crisp leaves that grow from the chicory root. Although traditionally grown in soil during the winter it is now also grown using

Below left *Mussels are the key component of Belgium's favourite national shellfish dish, and can be cooked in a variety of ways.*

Below middle *There are many different types of cheese available; some, such as this one, are mild and creamy, whereas others are hard and much stronger in flavour.*

Below right *Delicate, aromatic chervil is used in a range of dishes, from soups and salads to stews and sauces.*

hydroculture as a year-round crop. Connoisseurs, however, prefer endives grown the traditional way and will pay a little extra for this "white gold".

Belgium is potato country and cultivates a wide variety of the tuber, such as Bintjes, using them for many potato dishes including, of course, their adored *frites*. Fries are the most popular accompaniment to the national dishes of steak and mussels and will be served on a silver plate in top Michelin-starred restaurants, or in a traditional paper cone when eaten as street food with the fat dripping into the cone's base. Topped with mayonnaise or pickles the frites are devoured with finger-licking passion.

Herbs and spices

Although herbs such as parsley, tarragon, sorrel, chives, bay leaves, sage and thyme are regularly used, but the favourite is chervil, which is used for its aromatic, mild flavour in a range of dishes, such as eel in green sauce.

When the spice trade was at its peak during the Middle Ages, Belgian cooks integrated spices in their cuisine, but never excessively. Some spices are indispensable, though, and the Belgian pantry will always have nutmeg to use in the numerous potato dishes, sauces and soups. Saffron is a key ingredient in their national rice porridge dish, *rijstpap*.

The juniper berry is the only native spice and it is used for an array of game dishes and stews and to infuse the grain alcohol, *genever*. Cloves, ginger, vanilla and cinnamon are used sparingly in baking and desserts except when making the popular *peperkoek* (spice cake) and *speculaas* (spice cookies), when they are used generously.

Fruit

Apple and pear varieties, blueberries, cherries and sour cherries, peaches and plums are grown abundantly in the fruit region of Hageland and Haspengouw. Apples are used as an accompaniment to common dishes such as game, chicken and blood sausages, either as an apple sauce or a pan-baked side dish, or they will be cooked or baked with meat and vegetable stews to achieve the desired classic sweet-and-sour flavours.

Sour cherries are popular stone fruits and appear in many dishes, from *krieken met ballekes* (sour cherry compote with meatloaf or meatballs), to game and meat stews, *lapin a la kriek* (rabbit with cherry beer), and infused in *kriek* beers or as a topping for desserts. Excellent strawberries are also grown in several regions, and because they are of a high quality, are widely exported abroad.

Belgian pickles
Belgische pickles/pickles Belges

This combination of cauliflower, pickled cucumber and cocktail onions in a sweet-and-sour sauce is served with many dishes. Although store-bought varieties are available, this home-made one is worth the effort. **Makes 1 jar**

30ml/2 tbsp coarse sea salt (kosher salt)
100g/3³/₄oz/1 cup cocktail onions
100g/3³/₄oz/1 cup cornichons (small pickled gherkins)
100g/3³/₄oz/1 cup cauliflower florets

500ml/17fl oz/generous 2 cups white distilled vinegar or white wine vinegar
45ml/3 tbsp mustard powder
15ml/1 tbsp ground turmeric
5ml/1 tsp ground ginger
15ml/1tbsp cornflour (cornstarch)

1 Put the sea salt in a shallow bowl. Add the onions and cornichons and rub them with the salt until well coated. Cover and put in the refrigerator for at least 8 hours to draw off the excess liquid.

2 Next day, drain the vegetables and dry them with a clean dish towel. Cut the onions and cornichons into small pieces.

3 Bring a pan of lightly salted water to the boil. Add the cauliflower and cook for 3 minutes, until crisp-tender. Drain and rinse under cold water. Tip into a bowl and leave to cool, then mix with the onions and cornichons.

4 Pour the vinegar into a pan and bring to the boil. Meanwhile, mix the mustard, turmeric and ginger to a paste with a little water. Add to the boiling vinegar and stir until dissolved. Simmer for 5 minutes.

5 Mix the cornflour to a paste with 45ml/3 tbsp water. Add to the vinegar and cook, stirring, for 3 minutes or until thick. Remove from the heat and cool.

6 Pour the vinegar sauce over the vegetables and mix. Spoon into a clean jar, making certain that all the vegetables are submerged in the sauce. Close the jar and label with the date. When cold, store in the refrigerator for at least 14 days before opening.

Per jar Energy 365kcal/1527kJ; Protein 20.1g; Carbohydrate 39g, of which sugars 9.5g; Fat 22.9g, of which saturates 1.1g; Cholesterol 2mg; Calcium 235mg; Fibre 3.8g; Sodium 7888mg.

Condiments

Pickles, mayonnaise and mustards are Belgium's most beloved trio of condiments, indispensable at any Belgian table or pantry, and used to enrich appetizers, soups, meat and vegetable dishes and a multitude of sauces.

Pickles were developed as a way of preserving fruit and vegetables for the winter season, and Belgian pickles soon became a classic condiment. Combining gherkins, cauliflower and onions in vinegar, the recipe dates back to Roman times. When spices became more widely available turmeric was added, giving the pickles a vibrant yellow colour.

Belgians almost always serve mayonnaise with their *frites*. In addition, it is a classic base for many sauces, dips and other delicate culinary creations.

Hot-flavoured mustard became popular during the Middle Ages and every region in Belgium made its own version, distinguished by the use of regional seeds and flavourings. Today it is used in many classic dishes and to flavour mayonnaise, as a dip for *frites*, to season stews, to coat pork roasts or on bread accompanied with cheeses, hams or pâtés.

Bread

A variety of mixed grain loaves, bread rolls and a platter of assorted cold meats and cheeses can be a complete meal by itself in Belgium, where breads are devoured twice a day. Many daily expressions express the food's importance in the Belgian diet, such as "zijn broodje is gebakken" or "his bread has been baked" meaning "he has made his fortune".

Club sandwiches are popular brasserie or street food, and are often called *smos* or *smoske* (meaning "messy" in Flemish, because of the fact that the sandwich can become quite messy to eat). They generally consist of baguette-style bread layered with a choice of tomatoes, cucumbers, lettuces, meats, cheeses and egg or crab mixtures, depending on what is fresh and in season, spread with mayonnaise.

Chocolate

Belgium has one of the richest and finest chocolate traditions in the world, which adheres to very precise methods of chocolate processing, in which no preservatives, artificial flavours or colouring are ever used. As a result of these high standards, the chocolate is renowned for its exceptional quality.

Belgians take full advantage of this tradition and consume large amounts of chocolate in all kinds of different ways, including pralines, chocolate bars, candy, as part of countless desserts and sauces, and as chocolate spread served on bread.

Mayonnaise
Mayonnaise

Potato chips or fries are always served with mayonnaise in Belgium. The famous concoction of eggs, mustard, vinegar and seasoning can be plain or flavoured, and is also the basis of a wide range of dips, sauces and salad dressings. It is quick and easy to make. The secret of success is having all ingredients at room temperature. **Makes about 250ml/8fl oz/1 cup**

1 fresh egg yolk
5ml/1 tsp mustard powder or made mustard
15ml/1 tbsp lemon juice or white wine vinegar

salt and ground black pepper, to taste
120–200ml/4–7fl oz/1/2–scant 1 cup vegetable oil or sunflower oil

1 Mix the egg yolk, mustard, lemon juice or vinegar, salt and pepper in a bowl placed on a wet towel to prevent it from moving while whisking. Pour the oil into a jug (pitcher).

2 Whisk the mixture vigorously with one hand while adding the oil drop by drop with the other. When it begins to thicken, the oil can be added more quickly, in a thin and steady stream. It may not be necessary to add all the oil. Stop when the mayonnaise is thick and creamy. Check the seasoning, then transfer to a dish and serve immediately.

Per 250ml/8fl oz/1 cup Energy 958kcal/3940kJ; Protein 3.3g; Carbohydrate 0.5g, of which sugars 0.4g; Fat 104.8g, of which saturates 13.1g; Cholesterol 202mg; Calcium 27mg; Fibre 0g; Sodium 157mg.

Beer

Belgium is justly famous for the quality and variety of its more than 500 types of beer, produced in approximately 130 breweries. These range from popular pilsners, such as Stella Artois and Jupiler, to Lambic beers, brewed using natural wild yeast. These include Lambic, Gueuze, Kriek and Faro; Trappist and Abbey beers, like Chimay, Orval and Westvleteren; and a range of ales and red beers, to name but a few.

There are four different fermentation techniques, each of which results in a different type of beer. The temperature at which the fermentation occurs, the type of yeast used, whether the beer is filtered or not and the length of time it is left to ferment all affect the end result, and that is before the ingredients used or whether old and new beers have been blended has been taken into consideration. Ingredients may include fresh or stale hops, wheat, malts and fruit, such as cherries, which are used to flavour Kriek beer. The unifying characteristic, however, is that they all tend to be stronger than beers brewed elsewhere in the world, with an average alcohol content of about 7 or 8% abv.

Wine

Vines were planted in Belgium as early as the Middle Ages but disappeared on and off over the years because of vine disease, cold spells, invasions by rulers demanding the destruction of vineyards, and religious wars. However, the wine industry has made a comeback in modern times, producing good wines in the rolling southern hills of Hageland, Haspengauw and in Wallonia, made from grape varieties such as chardonnay, pinot gris, pinot noir and others. One of the best and largest Belgian wine makers, in the medieval castle Genoels-Elderen in Haspengauw, dates its history back to before 1700 and has been awarded the VQPRD (Vin de Qualité Produit Dans Une Région Déterminée), a label that certifies the wine is from a controlled source.

Liqueurs

The juniper-infused grain alcohol *jenever*, or *genever*, has medieval origins. The drink is usually drunk in a shot glass, referred to as a *borrel* or *witteke*. Certain *jenevers* are consumed in the morning, as was usual prior to the advent of coffee as the drink of choice, or it can be drunk as a nightcap on its own or mixed with a strong shot of espresso. It can also be used as a flavouring agent in cooking. Nationwide there are about 200 kinds of regional *jenevers* available, with a National Jenever Museum located in Hasselt, the capital city of the province of Limburg.

Belgian chocolate spread
Chocopasta/Pâté à tartiner au chocolat

Sweet and flavoursome, chocolate spread is a favourite breakfast food spread on freshly baked white bread rolls, delicious with a banana on the side and a glass of milk. Use chocolate with a cocoa solids content of at least 70 per cent. Callebaut is ideal. **Makes 800g/1¾ lbs**

200g/7oz dark (bittersweet) chocolate, broken into pieces
200g/7oz/scant 1 cup unsalted (sweet) butter, cubed

1 x 400g/14oz can sweetened condensed milk
finely chopped toasted hazelnuts (optional)

1 Put the chocolate in a heatproof bowl. Bring a small pan of water to the boil. Remove it from the heat and fit the bowl on top, making sure it does not touch the water beneath. Alternatively, use a double boiler.

2 Add the butter to the chocolate. Stir often to ensure the chocolate melts evenly. When the chocolate and butter have melted, stir in the condensed milk.

3 Add the finely chopped hazelnuts, if using, and stir until evenly distributed. Spoon into clean glass jars, cover and leave to cool. Keep in a cool place for up to 2 weeks.

Per 800g/1¾ lbs Energy 3840kcal/16016kJ; Protein 45.2g; Carbohydrate 350.2g, of which sugars 348.4g; Fat 260.8g, of which saturates 163g; Cholesterol 582mg; Calcium 1262mg; Fibre 5g; Sodium 1784mg.

Soups and appetizers

Belgians enjoy eating a wide range of soups and appetizers as part of a traditional lunch or dinner. Made with seasonal, often local, ingredients, they are carefully chosen so that they complement the courses that follow, and whet the appetite for what is to come.

Satisfying and elegant

Belgians are devoted soup eaters and every lunch or dinner in Belgium traditionally starts with a carefully selected soup made with seasonal ingredients. The history of soup can be traced back for centuries; historians state that the word "soup" derives from the old Germanic word *sop*, meaning "bread soaked in liquid". Many dialects in Belgium still refer to the food as *sop*. Until recently, villages and towns would have a *soep boer* (soup man), going from door to door with freshly made soup.

Every soup should begin with a good stock, a concept that dates back to times when all the bones and lesser cuts of meat or fish, as well as scraps of vegetables and herbs, were cooked in large cauldrons over an open fire to be made into nutritious communal meals called *potagie* – a one-pot soup, or a mash – such as the Flemish "hotchpotch" and *waterzooi* (soup or stew). Over the years, Belgian soups have evolved into refined concoctions, from consommés and velvety cream soups to seafood bisques and meaty winter warmers.

First courses and appetizers are usually light and simple, just enough to tempt the appetite before the courses that follow. Traditionally, a warm first course will be served before a simple meal, whereas a cold first course is more likely to be presented at meals with multiple courses.

Favourite ingredients include seafood from the coastal region, such as oysters, mussels and grey shrimp. These are lovingly transformed into an array of delectable combinations, ranging from shrimp-stuffed tomatoes and shrimp cocktail to shrimp croquettes and more.

Seasonal vegetables such as white asparagus and hop shoots are also popular, and are highly sought after during spring when they are available for only a limited amount of time. In the colder months, delicate cold cuts such as smoked and cured regional hams or other meat dishes, such as regional pâtés based on game, fish or other meats, will be infused with herbs, spices, wine or other spirits to make a tasty first course before a hearty meal.

Potato and leek soup

Aardappel preisoep/Soupe aux poireaux
et pommes de terre

Serves 4–6

25g/1oz/2 tbsp unsalted (sweet) butter
1 onion, thinly sliced
2–3 leeks (white and pale green parts
  only), thinly sliced and well rinsed
3 garlic cloves, roughly chopped
120ml/4fl oz/½ cup dry white vermouth
  or white wine (optional)
3 medium waxy potatoes, peeled and
  chopped small
1.5 litres/2½ pints/6¼ cups chicken or
  vegetable stock
3 sprigs fresh parsley
3 sprigs fresh thyme
1 bay leaf
200ml/7fl oz/scant 1 cup single (light)
  cream or milk (optional)
salt and ground white pepper
30ml/2 tbsp thinly chopped fresh chives
  or chopped parsley, to garnish

Leeks are a favourite Belgian vegetable, enjoyed on their own for their
pleasing subtlety and also indispensable as the basis of many soups.
Slightly tricky to clean, it is important that you wash leeks very carefully
before using them, as any grit that is not washed off can ruin a dish.
Smooth and creamy, this simple soup can be served warm as an
appealing appetizer or light meal, but is also delicious cold, as vichyssoise.

1 Heat the butter in a large, heavy pan over
a medium heat. Add the onion, leeks and
garlic to the pan and sauté gently for about
12 minutes, stirring occasionally, until
softened but not browned.

2 Increase the heat to high and pour in the
vermouth or wine, if using. Boil vigorously
for about 4 minutes, or until the mixture is
almost dry. Add the potatoes and stock.

3 Make a bouquet garni by tying the fresh
parsley, thyme and bay leaf together with a
piece of kitchen string (twine). Add this to
the soup.

4 Bring to the boil, lower the heat and cover
the pan, leaving the lid slightly ajar to let the
excess steam escape. Simmer for 20 minutes,
until the potatoes are very tender.

5 Lift out and discard the bouquet garni.
With a hand-held blender or in a food
processor, purée the soup until the desired
consistency is reached.

6 If using the milk or cream, whisk it into
the soup. Season and heat through.

7 Divide among warm soup bowls, garnish
with chives or parsley and serve immediately.

Per portion Energy 127kcal/534kJ; Protein 3.4g;
Carbohydrate 19.6g, of which sugars 3.9g; Fat 4.4g,
of which saturates 2.4g; Cholesterol 9mg; Calcium
40mg; Fibre 3.2g; Sodium 180mg.

Onion soup from Aalst

Aalsterse uiensoep/Soupe à l'oignon d'Alost

The region of Aalst in East Flanders has been known for its onions ever since mass cultivation started in the 19th century. Its inhabitants are accordingly nicknamed "ajuinboeren" (onion farmers) or "ajuine fretters" (onion gobblers). Onion soup has been touted as a good remedy for a hangover and is often served after New Year's Eve or Mardi Gras, both of which are enthusiastically celebrated in Aalst, which holds the most famous and oldest carnival celebration in Flanders.

Serves 4–6

50g/2oz/¼ cup butter
4 medium onions, (total weight about
   800g/1¾lb), chopped
4 garlic cloves, finely chopped
1 medium potato (about 200g/7oz),
   peeled and chopped
45ml/3 tbsp sherry or Calvados (if not
   using beer, see below)
1 litre/1¾ pints/4 cups vegetable, chicken
   or beef stock, or half stock and half
   beer (preferably Rodenbach)
1–2 sprigs fresh thyme
1 bay leaf
salt and ground black pepper, to taste
45ml/3 tbsp freshly chopped parsley,
   to garnish
freshly grated Gruyère cheese (optional)
hearty country bread or croûtons,
   to serve

Per portion Energy 146kcal/608kJ; Protein 2.5g, Carbohydrate 16.3g, of which sugars 8.1g; Fat 7.5g, of which saturates 4.4g; Cholesterol 18mg; Calcium 38mg; Fibre 2.2g; Sodium 339mg.

1 Melt the butter in a large, heavy pan and sauté the onions over medium high heat for about 10 minutes or until lightly caramelized. Add the garlic and sauté for 1 minute more.

2 Add the potato to the onions and stir well. If you are using sherry or Calvados instead of beer, add it to the pan at this point and let the mixture simmer for 3 minutes more.

3 Pour in the stock (or stock and beer) and add the thyme and bay leaf. Bring to the boil, reduce the heat and simmer for 35 minutes.

4 Remove the herbs and purée with a hand-held blender or in a food processor, until it reaches the desired consistency.

5 Season with salt and ground black pepper, to taste. Reheat if necessary, then ladle the soup into bowls.

6 Top each serving with freshly chopped parsley and add grated cheese if you like. Serve immediately with hearty country bread or croûtons.

Variation

Onion soup au gratin Place a generous amount of grated Gruyère in each soup bowl and top with a thin slice of toasted baguette before pouring in the hot soup. Sprinkle with a little more Gruyère and place under the grill (broiler) for 5–10 minutes, or until bubbly and lightly browned.

Serves 4

25g/1oz/2 tbsp unsalted (sweet) butter
1 white onion, chopped
3 garlic cloves, chopped
8 Belgian endives (chicory),
   cored and chopped
2 medium potatoes, peeled and chopped
1 litre/1¾ pints/4 cups chicken, veal or
   vegetable stock
500ml/17fl oz/generous 2 cups single
   (light) cream or milk
pinch of nutmeg
salt and white pepper

For the garnish

30ml/2 tbsp chopped fresh chives
   or dill sprigs
small endive leaves

Cream of Belgian endive soup
Witloof roomsoep/Soupe de crème d'endive

From appetizers and soups to entrées and side dishes, endives (or chicory, as the vegetable is known in the UK) are extremely popular in Belgium. Cream of Belgian Endive Soup is a classic dish from the region. It features on the menu of almost every festive meal and banquet, especially during the winter, since this is the traditional season for endives.

1 Melt the butter in a medium pan and sauté the chopped onion over medium heat for 5 minutes until it has softened but not browned.

2 Add the garlic and chopped endives and sauté for 5 minutes more. Add the potatoes and stock, bring to the boil, reduce the heat and simmer for about 30 minutes or until the potatoes are soft.

3 Pour in the cream and heat through. With a hand-held blender or in a food processor, blend until the desired consistency is reached.

4 Add nutmeg, salt and white pepper to taste. Reheat the soup if necessary.

5 Ladle the soup into bowls and garnish with the herbs and small endive leaves.

Variations
• Cream of endive soup can also be served chilled in ice-cold shot glasses for an elegant *amuse bouche*, served before the hors d'œuvre or first course of a meal.

• **Cream of endive soup en croute**
Have ready 4 sheets of puff pastry, cut to rounds slightly larger than your heatproof bowls, and 1 beaten egg. Ladle the soup into the bowls. Brush the pastry rounds with egg. Fit a pastry round over each soup bowl and crimp the edges. Place the bowls in a preheated 180°C/350°F/Gas 4 oven for about 10 minutes or until the pastry crust on each is golden. Serve immediately.

Per portion Energy 185kcal/778kJ; Protein 6.4g; Carbohydrate 24.6g, of which sugars 8.4g; Fat 7.9g, of which saturates 4.8g; Cholesterol 21mg; Calcium 172mg; Fibre 1.7g; Sodium 104mg.

Watercress soup
Waterkerssoep/Soupe au cresson

Watercress (*Nasturtium officinale*) and garden cress (*Lepidium sativum*) are nutritious aquatic leaf vegetables that grow wild alongside Flanders' cold river streams. Nowadays they are commercially produced to accommodate year-round demand. The peppery flavour of watercress makes it ideal for garnishes, sauces, salads and soups.

1 Heat the butter or oil in a large pan over medium-high heat. Stir in the onion, then sauté for 2–3 minutes. Add the leek, garlic and potatoes. Sauté for 5 minutes more, stirring until the mixture becomes fragrant.

2 Pour in the chicken or vegetable stock and add the bay leaf. Bring to the boil, reduce the heat to medium-low, cover and simmer for 20–30 minutes, until the potatoes are tender.

3 Stir in the watercress and garden cress. Simmer uncovered, for 3 minutes and no longer, to preserve the fresh green colour and cook the cress lightly.

4 Remove the bay leaf. With a hand-held blender or in a food processor, purée the soup until smooth or until it reaches the desired consistency. Season to taste with salt and pepper.

5 Reheat if necessary, ladle into warm bowls and serve, garnished with fresh watercress leaves.

Variation
Cream of watercress soup Add 120–200ml/ 4–7fl oz/½–scant 1 cup single (light) cream or milk with the watercress during the final 3 minutes' cooking.

Serves 4

25g/1oz/2 tbsp unsalted (sweet) butter
  or vegetable oil
1 large onion, chopped
1 leek, white part only, chopped
1 garlic clove, roughly chopped
2 large potatoes, peeled and cubed
1.5 litres/2½ pints/6¼ cups hot chicken
  or vegetable stock
1 bay leaf
1 large bunch of watercress, well rinsed,
  large stems removed, roughly chopped
1 large bunch of garden cress, well
  rinsed, large stems removed
  (see Cook's tip)
salt and ground black pepper to taste
60ml/4 tbsp watercress leaves,
  to garnish

Cook's tip
If you cannot locate garden cress, use 2 bunches of watercress.

Per portion Energy 598kcal/2515kJ; Protein 19.9g; Carbohydrate 76.3g, of which sugars 14.3g; Fat 25.9g, of which saturates 14.5g; Cholesterol 53mg; Calcium 602mg; Fibre 13.7g; Sodium 348mg.

Chervil soup
Kervelsoep/Soupe de cerfeuil

Chervil is a superstar in the Belgian kitchen repertoire. This versatile herb features in sauces, dips, compound butters, omelettes and garnishes, and is one of the five essential components in the classic *fines herbes* combination. It gives a subtle aniseed flavour to this delicate soup, which is an ideal introduction to an elegant dinner.

1 Melt the butter in a large pan over medium to high heat. Add the onion and sauté for about 5 minutes until fragrant and translucent.

2 Add the leek and potato and sauté, stirring constantly, for 5 minutes more.

3 Pour in the chicken or vegetable stock. Add the chopped chervil stems, bring to the boil, reduce the heat and simmer for 20 minutes or until the potatoes are tender. Add salt and pepper to taste.

4 Using a hand-held blender, food processor or a food mill, purée the soup until smooth. Stir in the chopped chervil leaves and cooked rice. Ladle into warm soup bowls and serve garnished with the chervil sprigs.

Variations
• Tiny meatballs can be added to the soup instead of the rice. In this case, add the chervil only when the meatballs are cooked.
• For a creamier texture, mix the chervil leaves with 60ml/4 tbsp crème fraîche before adding them to the soup.

Serves 4

25g/1oz/2 tbsp butter
1 onion, finely chopped
1 leek, white part only, finely chopped
1 large potato, peeled and chopped
1 litre/1¾ pints/4 cups hot chicken or
    vegetable stock
stems and leaves from 1 bunch fresh
    chervil (about 150g/5oz), chopped and
    kept separate, plus a few chervil sprigs
    for the garnish
50g/2oz/½ cup cooked white long
    grain rice
salt and ground white pepper to taste

Cook's tip
Although chervil stems can be cooked, the leaves are much more delicate. Avoid reheating the soup after adding them, if you can. If you must reheat the soup, use gentle heat and do not let it approach boiling point.

Per portion Energy 137kcal/573kJ; Protein 3.5g; Carbohydrate 17.6g, of which sugars 3.7g; Fat 6.3g, of which saturates 3.4g; Cholesterol 13mg; Calcium 98mg; Fibre 3.8g; Sodium 59mg.

Serves 4–6

30ml/2 tbsp vegetable oil
1 large onion, finely chopped
2 garlic cloves, crushed
2 carrots, finely chopped
2 celery sticks, finely chopped
1–2 small potatoes, peeled and chopped
800g/1¾lb ripe tomatoes, peeled, or
    2 x 400g/14oz cans chopped tomatoes
30ml/2 tbsp tomato purée (paste)
pinch of paprika
1 litre/1¾ pints/4 cups chicken stock
salt and ground black pepper
20g/¾oz vermicelli (optional)
chopped fresh parsley, to garnish

For the meatballs

250g/8oz/1 cup minced (ground) beef,
    pork or veal
1 egg
pinch of ground nutmeg
50g/2oz/1 cup soft white breadcrumbs
salt and ground black pepper, to taste

Per portion Energy 251kcal/1051kJ; Protein 13g;
Carbohydrate 23.5g, of which sugars 10.9g; Fat
12.4g, of which saturates 3.8g; Cholesterol 57mg;
Calcium 58mg; Fibre 3.6g; Sodium 320mg.

Tomato soup with meatballs
Tomatensoep met balletjes/Soupe de tomates
aux boulettes

Once regarded as peasant fare – a way of transforming leftovers into a
filling meal – soups are now in a culinary category of their own. This
tomato soup is the best-loved one by far, whether made with the utmost
simplicity or dressed up with brandy and cream.

1 Heat the oil in a large, heavy pan over
medium heat. Add the onion and sauté for
5 minutes, until softened but not browned.
Stir in the garlic, carrots, celery and
potatoes and cook over low heat for about
10 minutes, or until the vegetables soften.

2 Add the tomatoes and tomato purée, with
a pinch of paprika. Stir until the tomato purée
has dissolved, then pour in the stock and
bring to the boil. Reduce the heat, partially
cover the pan and simmer for 30–40 minutes.

3 Meanwhile, make the meatballs. Put the
meat in a bowl, then add the egg, nutmeg,
breadcrumbs, salt and pepper. Mix with
clean hands until the mixture holds together.

4 Roll the meat mixture into tiny balls – less
than 1cm/½ inch across – and set aside.

5 Purée the soup, using a hand-held blender
or a food processor. Return to the pan, if
necessary, and reheat. Season to taste.

6 Add the meatballs, with the vermicelli, if
using, and cook for 10 minutes on medium
high, until the meatballs are cooked. Ladle
into warm bowls and garnish each serving
with parsley. Serve immediately.

Variation
Stir in 200ml/7fl oz/scant 1 cup single (light)
cream towards the end of cooking, and heat
through for 3 minutes. Do not let it boil.

Flemish-style asparagus

Asperges op Vlaamse wijze/Asperges à la Flamande

Mechelen in northern Belgium is renowned for its white asparagus. With a unique, delicious flavour, the vegetable heralds the arrival of spring and its short season is celebrated with a range of soups, appetizers and other dishes. When it is not in season, green asparagus can be used instead.

1 Trim the asparagus spears or snap them so that the tender stalk separates from the tougher base. Soak the spears in a bowl of cold water, refreshing the water a couple of times; this makes the stalks more juicy and easier to peel.

2 Bring a large pan of lightly salted water to the boil. Peel the asparagus if necessary (see Cook's tip), and add the spears to the pan.

3 Blanch the spears for about 5 minutes (depending on the thickness of the stalks) or until they are crisp-tender.

4 Drain the asparagus and pat dry with kitchen paper. Arrange on individual plates or on a serving platter and cover to keep warm.

5 Heat the clarified butter in a frying pan for about 3 minutes, until pale brown. Add the chopped hard-boiled eggs, and season with salt and pepper.

6 Cook the mixture for 45 seconds, stirring constantly, then add the lemon juice. Pour the mixture over the warm asparagus, sprinkle with the lemon rind and freshly chopped parsley and serve immediately.

16 white or green asparagus spears
115g/4oz/½ cup clarified butter
4 hard-boiled eggs, finely chopped
grated rind and juice of ½ lemon
salt and ground black or
    white pepper
a handful of fresh parsley, chopped,
    to garnish

Cook's tip
Green asparagus seldom needs peeling but white asparagus has a tougher, woodier stem, so removing the tougher skin towards the base improves the texture and lets the stalks cook evenly.

Variation
Some cooks prefer to garnish the asparagus with alternate bands of chopped hard-boiled egg yolks – pressed through a sieve (strainer) – and finely chopped whites.

Per portion Energy 313kcal/1289kJ; Protein 9.3g; Carbohydrate 2.2g, of which sugars 2.1g; Fat 29.8g, of which saturates 16.6g; Cholesterol 252mg; Calcium 61mg; Fibre 1.7g; Sodium 245mg.

Marinated herring
Rollmops /Harengs marinés

Herrings have been a staple food in the Low Countries for centuries. Abundant, versatile and cheap, they can be prepared and served raw, cured, pickled or cooked. The term "rollmop" describes a herring fillet that has been rolled around a piece of pickled cucumber, fastened with a small wooden stick and marinated with onions and other flavourings in a vinegared brine. Partnered with a rye bread, mayonnaise and a refreshing cold beer, rollmops make an excellent snack or appetizer.

1 Rinse the herrings, pat them dry and set them aside. Bring the vinegar to the boil in a medium non-reactive saucepan. Add the salt, sugar, bay leaves and peppercorns, lower the heat and simmer for 5 minutes. Remove from the heat and leave to cool completely.

2 Place a cornichon widthways on each herring and roll up, using a cocktail stick (toothpick) to hold each rollmop together.

3 Place the rollmops in a clean glass jar, large enough to hold them snugly. Tuck the onion and lemon slices between the herrings.

4 Pour the vinegar mixture over the herrings to cover them completely.

5 Cover the top of the jar with clear film (plastic wrap) to prevent the vinegar from corroding the lid), then close the jar tightly.

6 Place in the refrigerator for 4 to 5 days, shaking the jar gently every day to redistribute the ingredients. Rollmops will keep for about 10 days in the refrigerator.

7 Serve with rye bread or wholegrain bread, home-made mayonnaise and lemon slices.

Serves 4

4 unsalted (sweet) herring fillets, cleaned and tails removed
400ml/14fl oz/1⅔ cups white distilled vinegar or white wine vinegar
15ml/1 tbsp coarse sea salt (kosher salt)
5ml/1 tsp sugar
2 bay leaves
4 black peppercorns
4 cornichons (small pickled gherkins)
1 onion, thinly sliced rings
1 lemon, thinly sliced
rye or wholegrain bread, Mayonnaise (see page 20) and lemon slices

Cook's tip
If using salted herrings, soak the fish overnight in a bowl of milk to remove the excess salt, rinse and pat dry. If you do not have time to do this, use the salted herrings without soaking them but omit the salt from the vinegar mixture.

Per portion Energy 94kcal/393kJ; Protein 7.7g; Carbohydrate 3.4g, of which sugars 3.2g; Fat 5.6g, of which saturates 1.4g; Cholesterol 21mg; Calcium 29mg; Fibre 0.2g; Sodium 52mg.

Tomatoes stuffed with grey shrimp

Tomaat met grijze garnaal/Tomates aux crevettes grises

This elegant Belgian classic is served at many restaurants and brasseries in summer, when tomatoes are abundant and at their peak. It also features top-quality Purus grey shrimps, which North Sea fishermen have for centuries caught and cooked at sea. Serve this as a first course to whet the appetite or as a satisfying lunch with crispy fries. An ice-cold local blond ale will balance the saltiness of the shrimp.

1 Slice the top off each tomato and set aside as lids. Using a spoon or melon baller, carefully scoop out the flesh, and either discard it or save it for making a soup or sauce. Season the inside of each tomato with salt. Stand upside-down on paper towels to drain.

2 Mix the lemon rind and herbs with the mayonnaise and season with salt and pepper to taste. Fold in the shrimps carefully, so as not to break them.

3 Spoon the shrimp mixture into each tomato and replace the caps, setting them slightly askew to reveal the filling.

4 Line a platter or individual plates with lettuce, watercress or mixed greens. Arrange the stuffed tomatoes on top and garnish each one with a twist of lemon and a sprig of parsley.

5 Surround with the remaining vegetables and serve.

Serves 4

4 medium unblemished tomatoes
grated rind of 1 organic lemon
15ml/1 tbsp chopped fresh parsley
  or chopped chives
60ml/4 tbsp Mayonnaise, preferably
  home-made (see page 20)
200g/7oz peeled cooked grey shrimps
  or pink salad shrimps
salt and ground black pepper to taste

To garnish

2 slices of lemon, halved
4 small sprigs of parsley

To serve

lettuce leaves, mixed greens
  or watercress
baby green peas, raw or lightly
  cooked radishes
alfalfa sprouts
grated carrots

Per portion Energy 186kcal/776kJ; Protein 13.2g; Carbohydrate 4.2g, of which sugars 4.2g; Fat 13.1g, of which saturates 2.1g; Cholesterol 76mg; Calcium 182mg; Fibre 1.5g; Sodium 1998mg.

Serves 4–6

24 large live mussels, scrubbed
and bearded
7.5ml/1½ tsp red wine vinegar or
lemon juice
30ml/2 tbsp vegetable or olive oil
1 shallot, finely chopped
1 spring onion (scallion), finely chopped
1 medium ripe but firm tomato,
finely chopped
salt and ground white pepper
30ml/2 tbsp freshly chopped parsley
and 4–6 lemon wedges, to garnish
crusty bread, to serve

Cook's tips

• Mussels for serving raw must be bought
from a reputable fishmonger so they are
guaranteed to be fresh.
• Marinated mussels can be kept in the
refrigerator for 4 days.

Marinated mussels
Gemarineerde mosselen/Moules parqués

Large, ultra-fresh cultivated mussels, served raw on the half shell in a
flavoursome vinaigrette, are a speciality of Brussels. They are particularly
popular around the time of *Brussel Kermis – Zuidfoor*, an annual summer
fair in the capital that lasts for one month, when locals and visitors are
invited to sample mussels and escargots at several spots in the city, to
celebrate the start of the new mussel season.

Per portion Energy 59kcal/246kJ; Protein 3.5g;
Carbohydrate 1.8g, of which sugars 1.1g; Fat 4.3g,
of which saturates 0.6g; Cholesterol 11mg; Calcium
14mg; Fibre 0.4g; Sodium 81mg.

1 Discard any mussels that are not tightly
closed, or which do not snap shut when
tapped. Holding a mussel firmly between
the thumb and index finger of one hand,
carefully lever it open from the side with a
sharp, short-bladed knife. Insert the knife
blade in the cavity and cut the muscle to
which the mussel meat is attached. Work the
knife blade around to free the mussel.

2 Put it in a non-reactive bowl. Repeat the
process with the remaining mussels. Wash
and dry the mussel shells and save them.

3 In a separate bowl, whisk the vinegar or
lemon juice with the oil. Season, then drizzle
over the mussels. Fold in the shallot, spring
onion and tomato. Cover and marinate in the
refrigerator for at least 1 hour.

4 To serve, arrange half the mussel shells
on a large platter and place a marinated
mussel on each. Garnish with parsley and
lemon wedges and serve with crusty bread.

Variation

Marinated cooked mussels Steam 24
prepared mussels until the shells open.
Discard any that remain shut. Remove the
flesh from the remaining mussels. Mix
together 100ml/3½fl oz/scant ½ cup white
wine, 5ml/1 tsp Tierenteyn or Dijon mustard,
1 finely chopped shallot, 2 crushed garlic
cloves and15ml/1 tbsp each of chopped fresh
parsley and chives. Season, then add the
mussels, cover and marinate for at
least 1 hour, stirring several times. Spear
on cocktail sticks (toothpicks), or put back on
to the half shells. Serve with lemon wedges.

Chicken fricassée in puff pastry baskets

Koninginnen hapje/Vol-au-vent à la reine

Serves 4-6

1 carrot, halved
1 onion, quartered
1 leek, thickly sliced
1 chicken, 1.3–1.8kg/3–4lb
2 bay leaves
1.5 litres/2½ pints/6¼ cups water
50g/2oz/¼ cup butter
50g/2oz/½ cup plain (all purpose) flour
200ml/7fl oz/scant 1 cup single (light)
  cream or milk
1 egg yolk
2 tbsp Madeira or sherry (optional)
juice of 1 lemon
8 bought or home-made vol-au-vent
  cases (see Cook's tip)
fresh sprigs of parsley or chervil,
  to garnish

For a meatball filling

150g/5oz/⅔ cups minced (ground) veal,
  pork or beef or a mixture
15ml/1 tbsp fresh white breadcrumbs
1 egg
salt and pepper

For a mushroom filling

15g/½ oz/1 tbsp butter
1 garlic clove, finely chopped
250g/9oz/3½ cups mushrooms, sliced

Cook's tip

If you prefer to make your own, smaller
vol-au-vents, you will need 450g/1lb puff
pastry, thawed if frozen. Roll out the pastry
to 5mm/¼in thick and stamp out 16 rounds
using a floured 10cm/4 inch cutter. Remove
and discard the centres from half the pastry
rounds, using a 7.5cm/3in cutter. Place the
complete rounds on a baking sheet and
brush around the edges with beaten egg,
then place a pastry ring on top of each.
Chill for ½ hour, then brush with beaten
egg and bake at 220°C/425°F/Gas 7 for
15–18 minutes until golden.

Per portion Energy 648kcal/2695kJ; Protein 37.8g;
Carbohydrate 22.6g, of which sugars 2.3g; Fat
46.1g, of which saturates 14.7g; Cholesterol 244mg;
Calcium 100mg; Fibre 0.8g; Sodium 345mg.

Little puff pastry baskets, also known as vol-au-vents, can be packed
with a range of delicious fillings, such as creamy chicken fricassée, tiny
meatballs or pan-fried mushrooms. They are served at all sorts of festive
occasions in Belgium, from Sunday lunch and anniversaries to birthday
parties and christenings. They are also standard offerings on brasserie
menus, enjoyed with fries and a cold beer.

1 Put the carrot, onion, leek and bay leaves
in a large pan. Place the chicken on top, pour
over the water and bring to a gentle boil.

2 Reduce the heat and simmer for about
1 hour or until the chicken is cooked. Lift
the chicken out of the stock and leave to cool.
Save the pan of stock.

3 When the chicken is cool enough to handle,
remove the skin and shred the meat from the
bones in bite-size pieces.

4 To make the meatball filling, mix the meat
with the breadcrumbs, egg and seasoning.
Form into balls 1cm/½ inch across.

5 Reheat the chicken stock, add the meatballs
and cook for 2–3 minutes, until they rise to
the surface. Remove the pan from the heat.
With a slotted spoon, transfer the meatballs
to a bowl, cover and keep hot.

6 For the mushroom filling, melt the butter in
a frying pan over medium-high heat.

7 Add the garlic and cook for 1 minute.
Add the mushrooms and cook for 5 minutes
more. Season, cover and keep warm.

8 Preheat the oven to the temperature given
on the packet of vol-au-vents or to 220°C/
425°F/Gas 7 if using home-made ones.

9 Melt the butter in a heavy pan. Add the
flour and cook, stirring, for 1 minute. Gradually
add the chicken stock, stirring all the time,
then add the cream. Continue to stir for about
8 minutes to make a thick and creamy sauce.

10 Remove from the heat and stir in the egg
yolk. Add the meatballs, mushrooms or
chicken with the Madeira or sherry, and lemon
juice and heat through. Adjust the seasonings.
Remove from the heat, cover and keep warm.

11 Cook the vol-au-vents for 15–18 minutes
or according to the instructions on the packet,
until golden. Place two on each plate and fill
with a filling of your choice. Garnish with
parsley or chervil sprigs and serve.

Snacks and street food

Whether bought from a street vendor or eaten in a café with friends, snacks are an integral part of the Belgian daily routine and there is a great range of treats on offer, from steak tartare and savoury pancakes to sumptuous waffles and fruity dumplings.

Toasted and tantalizing

For most Belgians, snacks are crucial breaks in the daily routine and rightly deserve the special status they have in its gastronomic repertoire. Numerous coffee houses, patisseries, brasseries and bakeries offer a large selection of savoury and sweet snacks throughout the day, and often stay open until late at night so that people can socialize there with friends and family in the evenings.

Pancakes and waffles with various toppings are especially popular, and are made at home or bought from one of the many establishments that specialize in them. Simple pancakes are served with a sprinkling of white or brown sugar, or with chocolate sauce or ice cream. The province of Limburg, however, is famous for its earthy buckwheat pancakes, which are often baked with bacon or apples and served spread with its artisan-made pear and apple syrup.

Classic *frites* are sold piping hot in a paper cone or served as an accompaniment to a main dish in a bistro or restaurant.

Specialist snack stands called *frietkots* are an iconic feature of Belgian towns and cities, and do a roaring trade at all times of the day. These convenient outlets used to sell only *frites*, but nowadays a multitude of other hot or cold snacks and drinks are offered there as well. Wherever they are sold, the crisp, golden fries are accompanied by the quintessential condiments, mayonnaise and Belgian pickles, or a variety of other popular sauces such as Andalouse, Béarnaise and tartare.

Despite the abundance and high standard of the mouthwatering treats available to buy on the streets, many Belgians enjoy rolling up their sleeves and making their own versions of their favourite foods at home, especially at the weekend when there is more time. Making the snacks from scratch not only increases the enjoyment and sense of satisfaction gained from eating them, but allows people to experiment with new ideas and adapt dishes to suit their personal preferences.

Serves 4

4 thick slices dark rye bread
15g/½oz/1 tbsp unsalted (sweet)
   butter, softened
200g/7oz/scant 1 cup Quark or sour cream
45ml/3 tbsp chopped fresh chives
1–2 shallots, finely chopped
salt and ground black pepper
8–10 red radishes, sliced paper thin,
   to serve

Cook's tip

Miniature versions of these snacks on small toasted bread squares make great finger food for serving with drinks.

Toast from Pajottenland

Platte kaas toost uit het Pajottenland/
Pain grillé du region de Pajotten

The area of Pajottenland in Brabant, to the west of Brussels, is famous for its unfiltered, naturally fermented *Geuze* and *Lambic* beers, as well as Belgian cheeses, such as "Pottekeis" a mixture of *platte kaas* (Quark or sour cream) and "Brusselse Stinkkeis" (literally translated to "stinky cheese from Brussels"). In this dish, Quark or sour cream is mixed with shallots, spread on slices of dark rye toast, and served with radishes and chives to counterbalance the tangy flavour of the cheese.

1 Toast the rye bread and spread with the softened butter.

2 In a bowl, mix the Quark or sour cream with 15ml/1 tbsp of the chives. Season with salt and pepper, then stir in the shallots.

3 Spread a thick layer of the cheese mixture on each slice of toast. Cover with radish slices to cover the cheese completely.

4 Season again with salt and pepper. Sprinkle with the remaining chives.

Per portion Energy 203kcal/845kJ; Protein 4.2g; Carbohydrate 17.3g, of which sugars 5.2g; Fat 13.6g, of which saturates 8.3g; Cholesterol 38mg; Calcium 80mg; Fibre 1.8g; Sodium 190mg.

Steak tartare on toast
Toost kannibaal/Toast cannibale

Steak tartare, as it is known elsewhere, is called *Filet Américain* in Belgium. It has also been dubbed "Toast Kannibaal" or "Cannibale", a reference to the fact that the meat used is raw. Every butcher's shop in the country prepares and sells this popular mixture, which is used to top toast, as a sandwich filling or spread on a baguette for the snack locals call a *Martino*. The key to a successful and, above all, safe steak tartare is to use only ultra-fresh beef of superior quality, and to chop it only at the very last minute. As a main dish, *Filet Américain* is usually served with fries.

Serves 4

2 fresh egg yolks
15ml/1 tbsp Dijon mustard
15ml/1 tbsp tomato ketchup
10ml/2 tsp Worcestershire sauce
Tabasco sauce, to taste
75ml/5 tbsp vegetable oil
2 shallots, finely chopped
30ml/2 tbsp capers, rinsed
6 cornichons (small pickled gherkins),
    finely chopped
30ml/2 tbsp finely chopped parsley
500g/1¼lb fresh sirloin steak, finely
    minced (ground) or finely chopped
    (see Cook's tip)
4 slices good quality white bread,
    toasted, crusts removed
15g/½oz/1 tbsp unsalted (sweet) butter
salt and ground black pepper
For the garnish
4 lettuce leaves
16 tomato slices
4 cornichons
4 parsley sprigs

Per portion Energy 538kcal/2237kJ; Protein 29.7g; Carbohydrate 20.4g, of which sugars 5.5g; Fat 38.3g, of which saturates 12.7g; Cholesterol 184mg; Calcium 84mg; Fibre 1.5g; Sodium 318mg.

1 Place the egg yolks in a large stainless steel bowl. Add the mustard. With a wire whisk, mix in the ketchup, Worcestershire sauce and Tabasco, with a little salt and pepper. Slowly whisk in the oil until the mixture is smooth. Fold in the shallots, capers, cornichons and parsley.

2 Add the chopped or minced (ground) raw meat to the bowl and mix well, using a spoon or clean hands. Shape into 4 patties by hand or use a small round mould.

3 Spread the toasted bread with butter. Place a patty of *Filet Américain* on each slice and press it down to cover the surface evenly.

4 Using a paring knife, score diamond shapes into the meat. Garnish 4 plates with lettuce leaves and top with the toast. Place 4 tomato slices alongside. Slice each cornichon lengthways, keeping one end intact, then fan the slices out. Place one fan on each slice of toast and garnish with a parsley sprig. Serve immediately.

Cook's tip
The preferred way of preparing the meat is by chopping it very finely with a sharp knife or cleaver. This gives the ideal texture. Alternatively, mince (grind) the steak with a mincer (grinder) fitted with a mesh blade. Don't use a food processor.

Herbed tansy pancakes from Diest

Kruidkoek uit Diest/Crepes aux herbes de Diest

The main ingredient in these pancakes – tansy – is a perennial flowering plant. Native to Europe and Asia, this aromatic herb enlivens anything from potato dishes to pancakes, puddings and omelettes. A speciality of the historic city of Diest in the province of Flemish Brabant, Herbed Tansy Pancakes are made in spring, when the tansy leaves are young and tender. The pancakes taste delicious served with cheese.

1 In a large bowl, whisk the flour, eggs, milk, melted butter and a pinch of salt to make a smooth batter. Fold in the chopped herbs.

2 Pour the batter into a jug (pitcher), cover and leave to stand for 1 hour so the flour absorbs more of the liquids.

3 Set a large non-stick frying pan over medium-high heat. When it is hot, grease it with butter. Off the heat, pour in enough batter to coat the pan generously.

4 Immediately tilt the pan and swirl the batter to coat the base. Tiny bubbles will immediately form on the surface. Set the pan back over the heat and cook the pancake for 1–3 minutes, until the surface looks dry and the edges are lightly browned.

5 Run a wide spatula under the pancake to loosen it. Turn it over and cook for 30 seconds more, until cooked through. Keep warm while cooking 4 more pancakes in the same way. Serve with slices of cheese.

Makes about 5

250g/9oz/2¼ cups plain (all-purpose) flour
2 eggs
500ml/17fl oz/generous 2 cups milk
50g/2oz/¼ cup butter, melted, plus
   extra for greasing
25g/1oz/½ cup finely chopped
   freshly-picked tansy leaves (not
   larger than 2.5cm/1in) or a mixture of
   dandelions, tarragon, parsley and dill,
   finely chopped
salt
a variety of aged cheeses, to serve

Cook's tip
Stack the cooked pancakes with baking parchment between each to prevent them from sticking. Wrap the package in foil and keep warm until ready to serve.

Per portion Energy 319kcal/1341kJ; Protein 9.6g; Carbohydrate 43.9g, of which sugars 5.7g; Fat 12.9g, of which saturates 7g; Cholesterol 108mg; Calcium 221mg; Fibre 2.1g; Sodium 112mg.

125g/4¼oz/1¼ cups buckwheat flour

125g/4¼oz/1¼ cups plain (all purpose)
   flour

7g/½ tbsp easy-blend (rapid-rise) dried
   yeast

30ml/2 tbsp sugar

2 eggs, at room temperature

500ml/17fl oz/generous 2 cups milk,
   buttermilk or Belgian ale, or an equal
   mixture of milk and water

salt

butter, oil or bacon fat, for greasing

1 eating apple, cored and cut into
   4 thick slices

pear syrup, for spreading

Per portion Energy 376kcal/1580kJ; Protein 13g;
Carbohydrate 58.2g, of which sugars 8g; Fat 12g, of
which saturates 6.1g; Cholesterol 119mg; Calcium
214mg; Fibre 1.9g; Sodium 136mg.

Limburger buckwheat pancakes
Limburgse boekweit pannekoek/Crêpes de sarasin

Villages in the Kempen are famous for their buckwheat pancakes, which
can be made with apple slices, bacon or brandy soaked raisins. They are
often served spread with the delectable pear syup that is produced in
Haspengouw, in southern Limburg and in Liège, an area renowned for its
pear orchards. If you are unable to find this thick, spreadable syrup then
you can use any pear syrup, although it may have a different consistency.

1 In a blender, a food processor or by hand,
whisk both types of flour with the yeast, a
pinch of salt, the sugar, eggs and chosen
liquid to make a smooth batter. Pour into a
jug (pitcher), cover and leave to stand for at
least 1 hour.

2 Just before cooking, stir to incorporate
any flour that has settled. The batter should
be thick but pourable. Set a 24cm/9½in
non-stick frying pan over medium-high heat.
When it is hot, grease it with butter, oil or
bacon fat.

3 Off the heat, place an apple ring in the
centre of the pan, then pour in enough
batter to coat the pan. Immediately tilt the
pan and swirl the batter to coat the base.
Tiny bubbles will form on the surface.

4 Set the pan back over the heat and cook
the pancake for 1–3 minutes, until the surface
looks dry and the edges are lightly browned.

5 Run a wide spatula under the pancake to
loosen it. Turn over and cook for 30 seconds
more, until cooked through. Keep warm
while cooking 3 more pancakes in the same
way. Serve with plenty of pear syrup.

Variations
Bacon buckwheat pancakes Grill (broil)
5 slices of rindless bacon until crisp. Place
1 slice in the centre of the pan, then pour in
the batter and cook as in the method.
Raisin buckwheat pancakes Soak 100g/3¾oz/
⅔ cup raisins in a bowl with 45ml/3 tbsp of
brandy or rum. Add to the batter and make
the pancakes in the usual way.

Makes 7-9 large waffles
....

500g/1¼lb/5 cups plain (all-purpose)
   flour, sifted
pinch of salt
15ml/1 tbsp easy-blend (rapid-rise)
   dried yeast
30ml/2 tbsp soft light brown sugar
5ml/1 tsp pure vanilla extract or
   1 x 8g/⅓oz sachet vanilla sugar
4 egg yolks, at room temperature
500ml/17fl oz/generous 2 cups
   sparkling water, whole milk or beer,
   at room temperature
200g/7oz/scant 1 cup unsalted (sweet)
   butter, melted and cooled
6 egg whites, at room temperature
icing (confectioners') sugar, for dusting
butter or whipped cream and/or chopped
   fruit, to serve

Cook's tip
Don't open the waffle iron during the
first few minutes of baking or the waffles
will separate.

Brussels waffles
Brusselse wafels/Gaufres de Bruxelles

These waffles are famous throughout the world, although the breakfast
food which many know as the "Belgian waffle" bears little resemblance
to the genuine article. Whether enjoyed at one of the many coffee or tea
houses or served at home after an afternoon of "*wafelen bak*" (waffle
baking), these light treats are always savoured. Recipes vary, but the basic
ingredients remain simple: flour, yeast and eggs mixed with milk, beer or
sparkling water. You will need a special Belgian waffle iron to make these.

1 Sift the flour and salt into a large bowl.
Stir in the yeast and sugar, with the vanilla
sugar, if using.

2 In a separate bowl, beat the egg yolks
with the milk or other liquid. Stir in the
vanilla extract, if using.

3 Make a well in the dry ingredients and
add the egg yolk mixture. Beat, gradually
incorporating the dry ingredients to make a
smooth batter. Stir in the melted butter.

4 Beat the egg whites until stiff peaks form
and carefully fold them into the batter.

5 Cover the bowl with clear film (plastic wrap)
and leave the mixture in a warm place for
45–60 minutes or until it has doubled in bulk.

6 Preheat a 17 x 9cm/6½ x 3½in waffle iron.
Pour in batter to the level recommended in
your instruction book (generally about three
quarters full) and bake for 4–5 minutes until
golden brown. The waffle should be crisp on
the outside and soft and airy inside.

7 Transfer to dessert plates and dust with
icing sugar. Serve with butter or whipped
cream and/or assorted chopped fruits so
guests can add their own topping.

Per portion Energy 444kcal/1856kJ; Protein 8.6g;
Carbohydrate 46.8g, of which sugars 4.5g; Fat 26g,
of which saturates 15.3g; Cholesterol 149mg;
Calcium 96mg; Fibre 1.7g; Sodium 215mg.

Serves 4

500g/1¼lb pack puff pastry, thawed
   if frozen
50g/2oz/¼ cup sugar
5ml/1 tsp ground cinnamon
4 crisp eating apples, such as Boskoop,
   Jonagold, Pippin or Granny Smith,
   peeled and cored
1 egg mixed with 15ml/1 tbsp water
icing (confectioners') sugar for dusting

For the filling

100g/3½oz/½ cup soft light brown sugar
ground cinnamon, to taste
25ml/1½ tsp cold butter, cut into
   small pieces

Cook's tips
• The dumplings can be made in advance
and baked shortly before serving.
• Cut out leaves or other shapes from the
pastry and use egg wash to fix them in
place on the dumplings before baking.

Per portion Energy 659kcal/2768kJ; Protein 9.1g;
Carbohydrate 92.1g, of which sugars 47.5g; Fat
32.1g, of which saturates 0.4g; Cholesterol 48mg;
Calcium 103mg; Fibre 1.2g; Sodium 409mg.

Apple dumplings from Antwerp
Antwerpse appelbollen/Boules aux pommes
d'Anverse

Whole crisp apples stuffed with brown cinnamon sugar and baked in
pastry are a speciality of the province of Antwerp. Along with sausage
breads, they are traditionally served on "Lost Monday." This annual holiday
takes place on the first Monday after Three Kings' Day (also known as
Epiphany) on January 6th, and the nickname "Lost Monday" derives from
the fact that workers are given a day off to celebrate.

1 Roll out the pastry on a floured surface
and cut it into 4 squares, each large enough
to wrap an apple easily.

2 Mix the sugar and cinnamon in a bowl and
roll each apple in it, to coat.

3 Preheat the oven to 200–220°C/400–425°F/
Gas 6–7. Place an apple in the centre of each
square of pastry.

4 Mix together all the ingredients for the
filling and use the mixture to stuff the cavities
of the apples.

5 Brush the edges of the pastry with
water, then lift the corners and bring them
together in the centre. Pinch the edges of
the pastry together with wet fingers, to
seal the seams.

6 Place on a baking sheet, spacing them at
least 2.5cm/1in apart, and brush with the
egg mixture. Bake for 20–30 minutes until
the pastry is crisp and golden.

7 Remove from the oven, and leave to cool
for 5 minutes. Transfer to individual plates, sift
icing sugar over and around the dumplings.

Fish and shellfish

Belgium is famous for its seafood and in particular for its national dish, *moules frites*. In addition to mussels, which are cooked in a variety of ways, Belgians enjoy many types of fish, including trout, cod, eel and monkfish, depending on what the fishermen have caught.

Light and aromatic

Because of the country's access to the North Sea, an exquisite seafood cuisine has developed over the centuries, and Belgian cooks are passionate about fish and shellfish. Ostend is the fish capital, providing the freshest catch of the day through the local fish markets.

Belgium's national dish, *moules frites* (mussels and fries), is eaten with gusto in homes and restaurants across the country. There are many different meticulous and creative methods of preparing the mussels, including steaming, marinating and poaching, but however they are cooked, they are always served with a generous helping of fries.

Belgium's grey shrimp are unique to the North Sea and are a celebrated ingredient, making a star appearance in a range of hot and cold dishes. In Oostduinkerke, age-old harvesting techniques are still used to collect these small crustaceans, whereby fishermen on horseback go into the shallow waters and drag nets behind them to scoop up the shellfish.

On the coast, numerous picturesque restaurants will offer a traditional speciality seafood menu offering the fresh fish of the day on their *dag menu* or *menu du jour*. These may include cod, monkfish, trout and eel, among others, and will be combined with herbs, cream and vegetables to create a range of appetizers, first or main courses, which are referred to as being *à la Flamande* (Flemish-style) or Ostend-style.

Among the many favourite national dishes is *waterzooi* (a soup or stew), which will be prepared with various sea fish, depending on what has been caught that day. Eel is also served throughout the country, with each region preparing its own speciality, including simply grilling (broiling) the fish and braising it with a good local beer or some white wine.

Numerous herring dishes are made throughout the country, either steamed, smoked, dried, grilled, baked or marinated and enjoyed simply with a piece of bread or a potato, fisherman-style.

Fish gratin Ostend style

Oostends vispannetje/Gratin de poisson à
l'Ostendaise

Ostend, a coastal town in the Flemish province of West Flanders, is
renowned for the quality of its seafood. The Fish Mine (*de Vismijn*) and
the Fish Market (*Vistrap*) offer the freshest catch of the day, which is put
to good use by local restaurants who feature classic dishes like this gratin.

1 Preheat the oven to 200°C/400°F/Gas 6.
Grease a 1.2 litre/2 pint/5 cup baking dish or
4 individual dishes. Cut the fish fillets into
even cubes, removing any stray bones.

2 Bring the fish stock to the boil in a large
pan. Add the fish cubes, reduce the heat
and poach for 2 minutes. If using scampi,
poach them for 1 minute, until barely pink.

3 As soon as the fish pieces are cooked,
lift them out with a slotted spoon and layer
in the dish or dishes. Season and cover
to keep warm. Pour the fish stock into a
measuring jug (cup).

4 Melt the butter in a pan over medium
heat. When it foams, whisk in the flour
and stir for 2 minutes.

5 Stirring all the time, add 500ml/17fl oz/
generous 2 cups of the reserved fish stock
in a steady stream, saving the rest to thin
the sauce later if necessary. Add the white
wine or vermouth in the same way. Simmer
for 3 minutes, stirring, then add the cream.
Season and simmer for 1 minute more.

6 Remove from the heat and add the grated
cheese, reserving 45ml/3 tbsp for the
topping. Stir in the grey shrimps and/or
mussels, with 15ml/1 tbsp of the parsley,
and spoon evenly over the fish. Sprinkle
with the reserved cheese.

7 Bake for 10–15 minutes, until the cheese
melts and turns golden. Sprinkle with the
remaining parsley and serve immediately
with crusty bread or potato croquettes.

Serves 4

400g/14oz firm fish fillets, such as
   monkfish, salmon, turbot or cod
200g/7oz cooked grey shrimps or/and
   shelled cooked mussels, or peeled
   uncooked scampi (extra large shrimp)
l litre/1¾ pints/4 cups fish stock
100g/3½oz/scant ½ cup butter
50g/2oz/½ cup plain (all-purpose) flour
100ml/3½fl oz/scant ½ cup dry white wine
   or dry vermouth
100ml/3½fl oz/scant ½ cup double
   (heavy) cream
115g/4oz/1 cup grated cheese
   (see Cook's tip)
45ml/3 tbsp chopped fresh parsley
salt and ground white pepper
crusty bread or potato croquettes, to serve

Cook's tip
Use a mixture of cheeses. Belgians use
a combination of local cheeses, but a
mixture of Gruyère and Parmesan cheese
also works well.

Per portion Energy 612kcal/2541kJ; Protein 36g;
Carbohydrate 10.5g, of which sugars 1g; Fat 45.3g,
of which saturates 27.9g; Cholesterol 190mg;
Calcium 358mg; Fibre 0.4g; Sodium 531mg.

90g/3½oz/7 tbsp butter

1 small onion or 3 shallots,
   very finely chopped

a handful of chopped fresh parsley

a drizzle of vegetable oil or olive oil

4 cod fillets, each about 175g/6oz

1 bay leaf

300ml/½ pint/1¼ cups white beer, such
   as Hoegaarden, or dry white wine

8 lemon slices

4 thyme sprigs

60ml/4 tbsp soft white breadcrumbs

To garnish and serve

chopped fresh parsley

lemon wedges

boiled or steamed potatoes

Cook's tip

This dish was once available only to those
who lived near the sea. Friday, the day
when Catholics eat fish, signalled the
arrival of the fish man in the villages, his
van filled with the catch of the day.

Per portion Energy 407kcal/1695kJ; Protein 27.5g;
Carbohydrate 13g, of which sugars 1.4g; Fat 25.3g,
of which saturates 12.5g; Cholesterol 111mg;
Calcium 44mg; Fibre 0.6g; Sodium 339mg.

Flemish-style cod

Kabeljauw op Vlaamse wijze/Cabillaud à la Flamande

Cod is one of Belgium's favourite types of fish, as it has a mild flavour
and plenty of dense, meaty white flesh that can be cooked in a variety
of ways. This recipe combines the fish with Hoegaarden white beer,
a refermented variety flavoured with ground coriander and orange peel.

1 Preheat the oven to 180°C/350°F/Gas 4.
Using half the butter, grease a flameproof
casserole or a frying pan that can be used
in the oven. Add the onion or shallots and
parsley. Drizzle with the oil. Transfer the
casserole or pan to the oven and cook
the onion for about 4 minutes.

2 Season the cod fillets on both sides. Place
on top of the onion and parsley mix. Add
the bay leaf and pour in the beer or wine
to almost cover the fish. Top each fillet with
2 lemon slices and a thyme sprig.

3 Return the casserole or pan to the oven
and bake for 15–20 minutes, depending on
the thickness of the fillets, until the fish
flakes when tested with the tip of a sharp
knife. Transfer the fillets to a platter, cover
with foil and keep warm.

4 Put the casserole or pan over medium
heat on top of the stove. Cook for about
5 minutes until the juices have reduced by
about three quarters. Add the breadcrumbs
and stir until they have been absorbed.

5 Cut the remaining butter into small cubes
and add to the sauce, a little at a time. Stir
until thick and creamy. If is too thick, add
more beer or wine to thin it. Check the
seasoning and pour the sauce over the fish.
Garnish with the parsley and lemon
wedges, and serve with the potatoes.

Variation

You can use whichever herbs you prefer
for this dish. A mixture of parsley, chopped
chives and dill works well, or you could add
a little tarragon (don't use too much, or it
will overwhelm the flavour of the fish).

Serves 4

....

4 medium fillets of monkfish
50g/2oz/¼ cup unsalted (sweet) butter
2 leeks, white parts only, finely chopped
25ml/1½ tbsp plain (all-purpose) flour
5ml/1 tsp mustard (optional)
300ml/½ pint/1¼ cups Belgian Abbey
   beer or dry white wine
1–2 tbsp capers, rinsed and dried
salt and ground black pepper
15ml/1 tbsp chopped fresh chives,
   chervil or parsley, to garnish
cooked potatoes or rye bread, and
   lemon wedges, to serve

Cook's tip
In Belgium a potato purée is often served with this dish, but boiled or steamed new potatoes or crusty rye bread would also taste delicious.

Monkfish in beer on a bed of leeks
Lotte in bier op een bedje van prei/Lotte en bière et poireaux

In Belgium, monkfish is called "Lotte" or "Zeeduivel". The latter means "devil of the sea" and refers to the ugly appearance of the fish. For a long time, superstitious fishermen believed that this fish brought bad luck and any that were caught were thrown back into the sea. Fortunately, the sweet taste and dense flesh has since earned it a place on the national menu.

1 Preheat the oven to 180°C/350°F/Gas 4. Rinse the fish fillets and pat them dry. Season both sides with salt and pepper, and set aside.

2 Melt the butter in a frying pan over medium heat. Add the leeks and sauté for 3 minutes. Add the flour and stir for 2 minutes until it has been absorbed.

3 Stir in the mustard, if using, and continue to stir while gradually adding the beer or wine to the pan.

4 When the sauce thickens, after about 5 minutes, season it, then scrape it into a baking dish. Level the surface.

5 Arrange the fish fillets on the sauce, and sprinkle over the capers. Cover the dish with foil and bake for about 30 minutes, or until the fish flakes when tested with the tip of a sharp knife.

6 Garnish with the herbs and serve with the potatoes or rye bread, offering the lemon wedges separately for squeezing.

Per portion Energy 268kcal/1125kJ; Protein 33.3g; Carbohydrate 2.6g, of which sugars 2g; Fat 11.6g, of which saturates 6.8g; Cholesterol 55mg; Calcium 65mg; Fibre 2.3g; Sodium 123mg.

Trout with almonds

Forel met amandelen/Truite aux amandes

The Ardennes region in the south of Belgium (Wallonia) is famous for its picturesque mountain scenery, deep valleys and cool, clear, forest streams. This is a popular destination for recreational fishing, especially during the trout season from mid-March to the end of September. Fresh trout is best cooked simply, to bring out its sweet flavour, and this classic method of preparation remains one of the best.

1 Rinse the trout under running water. Pat dry with kitchen paper. With scissors, cut away the fins. Turn each fish in turn on its back and ease open the cavity. Season inside and out and place 2 lemon slices and a quarter of the parsley in each cavity. Close with cocktail sticks (toothpicks).

2 Heat two 30cm/12in non-stick pans or oval fish pans over medium-high heat and add 15ml/1 tbsp oil to each.

3 Place two trout, skin side down, in each pan and sauté for 4 minutes, then turn over and cook for 3 minutes on the other side. As soon as the flesh becomes opaque and flakes when tested with the tip of a sharp knife, transfer to individual serving plates, using a large spatula or fish slice. Cover with foil.

4 Using one pan over medium high heat, pour in the wine and heat for 3 minutes, scraping the pan to incorporate the sediment.

5 Add the butter and a pinch of salt to the wine mixture. When it begins to brown, add half the almonds. Shake the pan over the heat for 5 minutes, taking care not to let the butter burn. When the almonds are golden brown, add the parsley and lemon juice.

6 Spoon the foaming butter and almonds over the warm fish and serve with extra lemon wedges and the remaining toasted almonds sprinkled over the top.

Variation

The trout can be dipped in flour before being fried, to give them a light crust, if you like.

Serves 4

4 whole trout, head and tail
   intact, cleaned
8 lemon slices
a handful of finely chopped flat
   leaf parsley
30ml/2 tbsp vegetable oil
100ml/3½fl oz/scant ½ cup dry
   white wine
115g/4oz/½ cup unsalted (sweet) butter
75g/3oz/1 cup flaked (sliced) almonds,
   lightly toasted
30ml/2 tbsp finely chopped fresh
   flat leaf parsley
juice of 1 small lemon
salt and ground black pepper
lemon wedges, to garnish

Cook's tip

If you prefer to use a thermometer to check that the fish is fully cooked, the interior temperature should be 60°C/140°F.

Per portion Energy 475kcal/1978kJ; Protein 39.2g; Carbohydrate 7.6g, of which sugars 0.8g; Fat 32.2g, of which saturates 12.4g; Cholesterol 187mg; Calcium 101mg; Fibre 1.2g; Sodium 249mg.

Eels in green herb sauce

Paling in het groen/Anguille au vert

The eels for this classic dish come mainly from the rivers Schelde and Nete, close to Antwerp, and restaurants all along the North Sea coast frequently feature it. Although recipes vary, the signature Belgian herbs chervil and sorrel, as well as spinach and parsley, are always used. These are added towards the end of the cooking time so their full flavour comes through.

1 Rinse the portions of eel and pat them dry with kitchen paper. In a small mixing bowl, mix together the egg yolks, lemon juice and water. Set the mixture aside.

2 Melt the butter in a large, heavy frying pan and sauté the shallots for 2–3 minutes over low heat until almost softened.

3 Meanwhile, strip the leaves from the thyme and put them into a mortar with the bay leaf. Crush with a pestle. Rub the mixture into the pieces of eel, then add to the pan. Sprinkle with salt and pepper.

4 Fry the pieces of eel on both sides for about 8 minutes until golden, then pour over the wine and enough fish stock to cover.

5 Cover and simmer for about 15 minutes, then lift out the pieces of eel with a slotted spoon and put them on a plate.

6 Remove the pan from the heat. Add the chervil, parsley and spinach, with the remaining herbs. Blend with a hand-held blender or in a food processor to chop the herbs further. Blend in the egg yolk mixture and add a little butter if necessary to thicken the sauce. Return to the pan if necessary.

7 Replace the pieces of eel in the sauce and warm through over a gentle heat. Stir until the sauce thickens but do not let it approach boiling point. Adjust the seasoning, spoon into a serving dish and garnish with lemon wedges and parsley. Serve warm or cold.

Serves 4–6

1.6kg/3½lb fresh small river eels, skinned, gutted and cut into 5cm/2in lengths (ask your fishmonger to do this)

2 egg yolks

juice of 1 large lemon

120ml/4fl oz/½ cup water

25g/1oz/2 tbsp butter, plus extra for thickening sauce if needed

2–3 shallots, finely chopped

1 sprig of thyme

1 bay leaf

300ml/½ pint/1¼ cups white wine

200ml/7fl oz/scant 1 cup fish stock

50g/2oz/1 cup fresh chervil, roughly chopped

50g/2oz/1 cup fresh parsley, roughly chopped

200g/7oz spinach, leaves torn and tough stems removed

15ml/1 tbsp each of chopped fresh sorrel, mint, sage, savory and tarragon

salt and ground black pepper

For the garnish

30ml/2 tbsp freshly chopped parsley

4 lemon wedges

Per portion Energy 290kcal/1213kJ; Protein 32.7g; Carbohydrate 1.9g, of which sugars 1.6g; Fat 13.4g, of which saturates 2.8g; Cholesterol 76mg; Calcium 218mg; Fibre 1.2g; Sodium 183mg.

Serves 4

4kg/9lb live mussels
40g/1½oz/3 tbsp butter, softened
2 onions, roughly chopped
3–4 celery sticks, roughly chopped
salt and ground white pepper
chopped fresh parsley, to garnish

To serve

fries or crusty bread
Belgian Pickles (see page 19), or
  Mayonnaise (see page 20)

Cook's tips
• Additional flavourings include leek or
carrot slices, chopped garlic, thyme and/
or bay leaves.
• A splash of white wine, poured over the
mussels before cooking, improves the dish,
and a little hot mustard can also be added.
• The pan juices are delicious, so give
diners spoons as well as bread for mopping.

Per portion Energy 393kcal/1658kJ; Protein 46.5g;
Carbohydrate 17.3g, of which sugars 6g; Fat 15.5g,
of which saturates 6.2g; Cholesterol 181mg;
Calcium 183mg; Fibre 1.9g; Sodium 1048mg.

Steamed mussels with celery
Mosselen natuur/Moules marinière

One of the best ways of preparing this national dish is to simply steam the
mussels in their own juices with celery and onions: *à la Marinière* or *à la
Nature*. This allows the delectable flavour of the mussels to shine through.
In Belgium, the mussels are traditionally served in individual casseroles
whose lids can be inverted to make a container for the empty shells.

1 Scrub the mussels until the shells are
shiny black and smooth. Remove beards,
if present. If any of the shells are cracked
or broken, discard them, along with any
mussels that are open and that do not snap
shut if tapped.

2 Melt the butter in a large heavy pan over
medium heat. Add the onions and sauté for
5 minutes until softened and glazed. Add
the celery and sauté for 5 minutes more.
Add the mussels and season generously
with salt and pepper.

3 Cover the pan and place over high heat
for 3–4 minutes or until the mussels open,
shaking the pan occasionally to distribute
the steam.

4 Discard any mussels that have failed to
open. Taste the liquid in the pan and adjust
the seasoning if necessary, then spoon the
mussels and the liquid into bowls or pots.

5 Sprinkle with parsley and serve with fries
or crusty bread. Offer pickles, mayonnaise
or mustard vinaigrette on the side.

Poultry and game

Chicken, pheasant, partridge, duck, rabbit and venison are celebrated in a number of warming and hearty dishes in Belgium, including roasts, stews and braises, often combined with local beer and a range of vegetables.

Flavoursome and sustaining

Flanders is home to many traditional quality poultry breeders, and many Belgians have chickens roaming in designated areas of their gardens or grounds, giving them succulent poultry for cooking. As a result, chicken is a favourite at the dinner table. Once reserved solely for Sundays, it is now eaten much more frequently in a range of dishes, including a classic roast served with apple sauce and potato croquettes or *frites,* the well-known *vol au vent* and in the national soup or stew, *waterzooi.*

During the Burgundian era, lavish banquets were frequently arranged for kings and nobles, with long tables laden with dishes made from pheasants, capons, doves, partridges, swans, wild ducks, venison, wild boar, hare and other animals that roamed the Belgian forests.

Many of these ancient recipes have survived and a range of stews, braises and roasts are still enjoyed in the home and restaurants during the hunting season, especially in the Ardennes region where the game is most prolific.

Wild boar has played an important role in the Belgian diet since Celtic times, when domestic pigs were allowed to run around freely in the streets. These pigs often wandered off into the oak forests and eventually their descendants became wild boars, thriving on an excellent diet of acorns, roots, grass, fruits and mushrooms, which gave their meat a distinctive taste. The tradition of preparing and eating wild boar meat is devotedly observed in the Ardennes, where it is made into delectable sausages, salamis, smoked hams, ragoûts and stews.

Rabbit and hare are also still cooked in traditional stews, flavoured with local beers, fruits and spices. This combination of ingredients harks back to medieval times, when spices were first brought back from the far east and incorporated into the dishes. The addition of fruit helps to cut through any fattiness from the meat, and adds the distinctive sweet-sour flavour that characterizes many of the dishes that are enjoyed throughout the country.

Chicken with forest mushrooms

Mechelse koekoek met bos paddestoelen/Coucou de malines aux champignons du bois

This delicious stew dates from a time when chicken was a rare treat, and was traditionally served in autumn, when wild mushrooms were abundant. Abbey beer and a locally distilled *genever* make it extra special.

1 Cut the chicken in 4 or 6 pieces and season with salt and pepper. Coat lightly with flour, shaking off the excess.

2 Melt 30ml/2 tbsp of the butter with 15ml/ 1 tbsp of the oil in a large heavy frying pan. Add the chicken and brown on both sides over medium heat for about 10 minutes or until golden. Lift out and put into a bowl.

3 Sauté the onions in the fat remaining in the pan for 3 minutes or until translucent. Stir in the garlic and mushrooms and fry for about 5 minutes, adding more butter and oil as needed, until the onions are golden. Stir in the *genever* or gin and cook for 2 minutes more, to reduce slightly.

4 Using a slotted spoon, scoop out the onion mixture and add it to the chicken.

5 Add the sugar and vinegar to the pan and whisk over medium heat for 1–2 minutes or until dissolved. Return the chicken and vegetables to the pan and pour over the chicken stock and beer.

6 Tuck the bouquet garni among the chicken pieces, cover and simmer over low heat for 1 hour, until the chicken falls off the bone.

7 With a slotted spoon, transfer the chicken and vegetables to a heated serving platter. Discard the bouquet garni. Cover the chicken with foil to keep it warm.

8 Skim the fat from the surface of the sauce, then boil it for 5 minutes, until reduced by about one-third. Check the seasoning, pour the sauce over the chicken and serve.

Serves 4–6

1 good quality chicken, about 1.6kg/3½lb
15g/½oz/2 tbsp plain (all-purpose) flour
40g/1½oz/3 tbsp butter
30ml/2 tbsp vegetable oil or olive oil
3 onions, halved and sliced
1 garlic clove, crushed
450g/1lb/6 cups wild mushrooms, sliced
30ml/2 tbsp *Hasseltse genever* or gin
15ml/1 tbsp soft light brown sugar
30ml/2 tbsp red wine vinegar
100ml/3½fl oz/scant ½ cup chicken stock
500ml/17fl oz/generous 2 cups
   Abbey beer
1 bouquet garni (see page 70)
salt and ground black pepper

Cook's tip

Belgian gastronomes rave about *Mechelse koekkoek*, or *Coucou de Malines*, a breed of chicken from Mechelen with a fabulous flavour. This is due to the fact that it doesn't have a true fat layer. Instead, fat stores are distributed throughout the meat, making it juicy and tender. If you can't buy this type of chicken, use any good quality bird.

Per portion Energy 563kcal/2336kJ; Protein 33.2g; Carbohydrate 10.2g, of which sugars 6.6g; Fat 40.9g, of which saturates 12.1g; Cholesterol 174mg; Calcium 44mg; Fibre 1.8g; Sodium 177mg.

Ghent-style chicken stew
Gentse waterzooi/Waterzooi de poulet à la Gantoise

Waterzooi (meaning boiled or stewed in water), is a centuries-old soup or stew that is associated with the city of Ghent, the capital of East Flanders. Originally prepared with fish from the city's network of rivers and canals, the chicken version has now become the more popular choice.

1 Rinse the chicken and trim off any excess fat. Place the whole bird in a large pot and pour over chicken stock to two-thirds cover. Add the thyme, bay leaves, clove, peppercorns and crushed garlic. Bring to the boil.

2 Reduce the heat, cover and simmer for 1–1½ hours or until the chicken is cooked and the meat begins to fall from the bones.

3 Lift the chicken out of the pan. When it is cool enough to handle, remove the skin, take the meat off the bones and cut it into bite-size pieces. Put these in a bowl, cover and set aside. Skim the fat from the surface of the stock, then pour it into a large jug (pitcher) and set aside.

4 Melt the butter in the clean pan. Add all the vegetables except the potatoes and fry over a low heat for 10 minutes, stirring frequently, until softened. Pour in the reserved stock and the potatoes, bring to the boil and cook for 10–15 minutes, until the potatoes are tender.

5 Mix the egg yolks and cream in a bowl. Remove the pan from the heat and gradually stir the cream mixture into the soup/stew. Add the chicken pieces. Return to the heat and cook, stirring constantly for 5 minutes, until thickened. Do not let it boil.

6 Season with salt, pepper and nutmeg. Add lemon juice if you like. Ladle into bowls, sprinkle with parsley and serve immediately.

Serves 4–6

1 free-range (farm-fresh) chicken, about 1.6kg/3½lb
chicken stock, to cover the meat (see method)
2 sprigs of thyme
2 bay leaves
1 clove
10 peppercorns
1 garlic clove, crushed
40g/1½oz/3 tbsp unsalted (sweet) butter or vegetable oil
3 carrots, finely chopped
2 onions, finely chopped,
2 leeks, white part only, thinly sliced
¼ celeriac or 2 celery sticks, finely chopped
6 small potatoes, quartered
2 egg yolks
200ml/7fl oz/scant 1 cup double (heavy) cream
salt and ground black pepper
pinch of grated nutmeg
lemon juice for squeezing (optional)
a handful of fresh parsley, chopped, to garnish

Per portion Energy 660kcal/2739kJ; Protein 33.7g; Carbohydrate 16.7g, of which sugars 1.9g; Fat 51.3g, of which saturates 22.7g; Cholesterol 287mg; Calcium 44mg; Fibre 1g; Sodium 187mg.

Brabant-style pheasant

Fazant op Brabantse wijze/Faison à la Brabançonne

Serves 4

15ml/1 tbsp vegetable oil, plus extra
    for greasing
2 young pheasants, cleaned and pan ready
115g/4oz/½ cup butter
200g/7oz bacon slices
8 Belgian endives (chicory), cores and
    any tough outer leaves removed
pinch of sugar
salt and ground black pepper
celeriac or parsnip purée, to serve

Cook's tips
• Wrapping the pheasant in bacon will help
to keep it moist while roasting.
• If you wish to test the pheasants with a
meat thermometer, the internal temperature
when they are cooked should be 65°C/149°C.

Per portion Energy 896kcal/3738kJ; Protein 90.4g;
Carbohydrate 1.9g, of which sugars 1.9g; Fat 58.7g,
of which saturates 26.5g; Cholesterol 88mg;
Calcium 160mg; Fibre 0.9g; Sodium 1211mg.

In the Middle Ages, when hunting was a favourite pursuit of the wealthy
and game was reserved for nobles, pheasant tended to be served only
at upper class tables. Today, the bird has wider appeal and dishes like this
one often feature on gastronomic menus in the Ardennes, especially
during the shooting season in autumn. Wild pheasants are the best option,
but farmed birds, which have a less gamey flavour, can be used instead.

1 Preheat the oven to 180°C/350°F/Gas 4.
Grease a roasting pan lightly with oil.
Season the pheasants generously inside and
out with salt and pepper. Put 2.5ml/½ tsp
butter in the cavity of each bird.

2 Heat 60ml/4 tbsp of the remaining butter
with the oil in a heavy frying pan which is
large enough to hold both pheasants. Add
the birds, placing them on their sides. Fry
over medium heat for about 10 minutes,
turning the pheasants until they are golden
brown on all sides.

3 Lift out the birds and set the pan aside.
When the birds are cool enough to handle,
wrap them in bacon, tying it on with kitchen
string (twine). Put the pheasants in the
greased roasting pan, cover with foil or a lid,
and roast in the oven for 45 minutes.

4 Meanwhile, return the frying pan to the
heat, reheat the fat, then add the endives
in a single layer. Pour in enough water to
come halfway up the endives. Dot with
5ml/1 tsp butter and season with salt and
pepper. Bring to the boil, reduce the heat,
cover and simmer for 20 minutes.

5 Using tongs, turn the endives over, replace
the lid and simmer for 15–20 minutes more,
until tender all the way through.

6 When the pheasants are done remove
them from the roasting pan and put them on
a chopping board. Slit the string, remove the
bacon and set it aside, then cover the birds
with foil and leave to rest for 10 minutes.

7 Lift the endives out of the frying pan and
put them on a plate. Pour their cooking
liquid into the roasting pan. Place over
medium-high heat and boil, stirring frequently,
for 8 minutes. Meanwhile, return the endives
to the frying pan, sprinkle with the sugar
and cook until caramelized on both sides.

8 Add the remaining butter to the reduced
sauce in the roasting pan and stir over the
heat for 4 minutes or until it thickens.
The reserved bacon can be chopped or
crumbled and added to the sauce, if you like.

9 Carve the birds and arrange on a heated
platter. Arrange the endives around the meat
and spoon the sauce over. Serve with the
celeriac or parsnip purée.

Braised partridge with cabbage

Patrijs met groene kool uit St. Hubert/Perdrix au chou vert de St. Hubert

For this classic dish from the historic city of Saint Hubert, partridges are layered with Savoy cabbage or Brussels sprouts and cooked in stock and Abbey beer. You can use wild or farmed partridges.

1 Cut each partridge in half down the centre. Season with salt and pepper.

2 Melt the butter in a large heavy frying pan over medium-high heat. Add the partridge halves and brown them on both sides. Cover the pan with foil or a lid and cook over low heat for 30 minutes.

3 Meanwhile, bring a large pan of water to the boil. Stir in 15ml/1 tbsp salt. Add the cabbage and blanch it for 3 minutes, then drain and pat dry with kitchen paper.

4 Lift the partridges out of the frying pan and put them on a plate. Set aside. Reheat the fat in the pan and add the bacon and both types of sausage. Fry, stirring occasionally for 5 minutes, until the bacon is crisp and the sausages are fully cooked.

5 Preheat the oven to 160°C/325°F/Gas 3. Grease a baking dish that is large enough to hold the pheasant halves in a single layer. Spread half the cabbage on the base and season it with salt, pepper and nutmeg.

6 Place the partridges on top and arrange the bacon and sausages in between. Cover with the rest of the cabbage and season again with salt, pepper and nutmeg.

7 Pour over the hot chicken stock and beer (or both quantities of stock). Add the bay leaves and juniper berries, cover the dish and bake in the oven for 1 hour.

8 Adjust the seasoning. Mound the cabbage on a heated platter and arrange the partridges on top, with the bacon and sausages around the side. Serve with the potatoes.

Serves 4

2 mature partridges, cleaned and ready to cook
115g/4oz/½ cup butter
1 large Savoy cabbage, sliced
200g/7 oz rindless smoked streaky (fatty) bacon
4 small pork sausages
4 small smoked sausages
pinch of freshly grated nutmeg
250ml/8fl oz/1 cup hot chicken stock
750ml/1¼ pints/3 cups dark Abbey beer or more hot chicken stock
2 bay leaves
4 juniper berries
salt and ground black pepper
boiled or mashed potatoes, to serve

Per portion Energy 1016kcal/4227kJ; Protein 79.7g; Carbohydrate 15.2g, of which sugars 10g; Fat 66.2g, of which saturates 29g; Cholesterol 139mg; Calcium 219mg; Fibre 2.9g; Sodium 1633mg.

4 duck breasts, skin on
15ml/1 tbsp clear honey
1kg/2¼lb fresh young turnips
50g/2oz/¼ cup unsalted (sweet) butter
15ml/1 tbsp sherry vinegar
salt and ground pepper
chopped fresh chervil or parsley,
   to garnish

Cook's tips
• Select duck breast that has a fatty skin,
as this will protect the meat from drying
out when pan-frying.
• Cook duck breast like you would a fine
filet mignon – so that it is pink and tender
in the middle.

Per portion Energy 591kcal/2446kJ; Protein 13.7g;
Carbohydrate 14.7g, of which sugars 14.2g; Fat
53.7g, of which saturates 18.1g; Cholesterol 27mg;
Calcium 134mg; Fibre 6g; Sodium 191mg.

Duck breast with turnips
Eendeborst met raapjes/Canard aux navets

Whether wild or farmed, duck is often served at festive occasions in
Belgium. In this recipe, duck breasts are combined with turnips, an ancient
root vegetable that has been widely used for centuries – it was a staple in
many medieval stews and hotpots before the arrival of the potato.

1 Rinse the duck breasts and pat them dry
with kitchen paper. Trim off any sinew. Using
a sharp knife, cross hatch the fatty skin on
each breast and rub with honey on both
sides. Take care to cut right through the fatty
skin without piercing the meat.

2 Scrub, rinse and dry the turnips and slice
them thinly. Melt the butter in a frying pan
over medium-high heat. Add the turnips and
fry for 10 minutes, stirring occasionally until
they start to brown.

3 Meanwhile, put the duck breasts, skin-side
down, in a large non-stick frying pan. Cook
over medium heat for about 5 minutes or
until the fat runs and the skin becomes crisp
and golden.

4 Drain off any excess fat from the duck
breasts, if necessary. Season to taste.

5 Using tongs, turn the duck breasts over
and cook the other side for 5–6 minutes.
Do not overcook. Season again. Remove
from the heat, cover with foil or a lid and set
aside for 4–5 minutes.

6 Add the sherry vinegar to the turnips
and stir over the heat for 3 minutes until
reduced. Season to taste and spoon on to
warm plates.

7 Slice the duck breasts thinly and fan over
the turnips, spooning a little of the juices
from the pan on top. Garnish with the
chopped herbs and serve.

Rabbit in cherry beer
Konijn in kriek bier/Lapin à la kriek

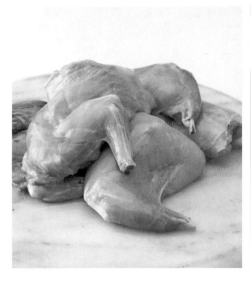

Serves 4

1 ready-to-cook rabbit, cut in four pieces
40g/1½oz/3 tbsp butter
15ml/1 tbsp vegetable oil
1 large onion, roughly chopped
2 carrots, finely chopped
2 celery sticks, finely chopped
2 bay leaves
3 sprigs of thyme
10 peppercorns
250ml/8fl oz/1 cup Kriek Lambic beer
15ml/ tbsp clear honey
1 x 470g/1lb ¾oz can or jar sour cherries
    in syrup (see Cook's tip)
15ml/1 tbsp red wine vinegar
salt and ground black pepper
50g/2oz/½ cup plain (all-purpose) flour
parsley sprigs, to garnish
boiled potatoes, potato croquettes or
    crusty dark bread, to serve

Cook's tips
• If you cannot locate sour cherries labelled as such, buy canned or bottled Morello cherries.
• Kriek Beer is now widely available outside Belgium.

Per portion Energy 471kcal/1975kJ; Protein 32.7g; Carbohydrate 39.1g, of which sugars 27.2g; Fat 19.6g, of which saturates 9g; Cholesterol 168mg; Calcium 75mg; Fibre 2.4g; Sodium 111mg.

Rabbit and hare are central to Belgian cuisine. There are hundreds of ways of cooking them, often with traditional beers, fresh or dried fruits, spices and locally produced mustards. This recipe comes from the Brussels area, where Kriek (sour cherry) beer is produced. In combination with the canned sour cherries, the beer gives the slow-cooked dish a sweet-sour flavour that echoes the cooking style of Belgium's medieval past. There isn't a lot of meat on a rabbit, so you should ask for one to serve four when buying it.

1 Season the pieces of rabbit with salt and pepper. Melt 30ml/2 tbsp of the butter in a large, heavy frying pan over medium heat. When it foams, add the oil. Add the pieces of rabbit and fry, turning occasionally, for 8 minutes or until browned on all sides. Lift out the rabbit and place on a platter.

2 Add the onion to the fat remaining in the pan. Sauté for 3–4 minutes until glazed then stir in the carrots and celery. Continue cooking, stirring constantly over medium heat, for about 12 minutes, until the vegetables have browned slightly.

3 Return the rabbit to the pan and spoon the vegetables over. Season again. Tuck the bay leaves, thyme and peppercorns among the rabbit portions.

4 Pour over the beer, honey and vinegar to just cover the rabbit and vegetables. Add a little of the syrup from the canned cherries, if you like.

5 Cover and simmer for 1 hour or until the rabbit meat starts to fall off the bones.

6 Lift out the rabbit pieces and put them on a heated serving platter. Cover to keep warm. Remove the vegetables and herbs with a slotted spoon and discard them.

7 Reheat the pan juices and sprinkle over the flour. Cook for 1 minute, stirring constantly to incorporate all the brown bits from the base of the pan. Cook the sauce, stirring frequently, until reduced by half.

8 Drain the cherries, reserving the syrup, and stir them in. Simmer for 10 more minutes. Add a little of the syrup to thin the sauce, if necessary. Swirl the remaining butter into the sauce. Return the pieces of rabbit to the pan and reheat gently in the sauce.

9 Taste and adjust the seasoning and serve at once with boiled potatoes, potato croquettes or crusty dark bread.

Ardennes-style venison stew

Wild ragout uit de Ardennen/Civet à l'Ardennaise

Serves 4–6

1.6kg/3½lb stewing venison, cubed
150g/5oz bacon bits (optional)
25g/1oz/2 tbsp butter
15ml/1 tbsp vegetable oil or olive oil
1 onion, finely chopped
15g/½oz/2 tbsp plain (all purpose) flour
45ml/3 tbsp brandy
150g/5oz packet dried mixed
    wild mushrooms
bouquet garni (see Cook's tip)
15ml/1 tbsp cornflour (cornstarch), mixed
    to a paste with 45ml/3 tbsp water
30ml/2 tbsp red wine vinegar

For the marinade

1 onion, roughly chopped
1 carrot, roughly chopped
2 garlic cloves, crushed
20 juniper berries
3 bay leaves
4 cloves
1 sprig of thyme
1 litre/1¾ pints/4 cups red wine
15ml/1 tbsp vegetable or olive oil

To serve

Poached Apples with Berry Compote
    (see page 89)
boiled new potatoes with butter and
    chopped parsley

Cook's tip

To make the bouquet garni, tie 6 parsley
sprigs, 2 bay leaves and 2–3 fresh sprigs
of thyme together with kitchen string
(twine). Leave a trailing end long enough
to tie to the pan handle, so that the
bouquet garni can easily be retrieved.

Per portion Energy 474kcal/1996kJ; Protein 60.7g;
Carbohydrate 8.7g, of which sugars 3.3g; Fat 9.6g,
of which saturates 4.3g; Cholesterol 142mg;
Calcium 44mg; Fibre 1.1g; Sodium 188mg.

November is prime game season in Belgium. Months before, lovers of good food go on gastronomic weekends in the Belgian Ardennes so that they can sample the superb dishes that are only available at this time. Game is often marinated in wine and spices before being cooked. This way of preserving and tenderizing meat is one of the world's oldest culinary techniques. It is used to great advantage in this delectable stew, promoting complex flavours and tempting aromas.

1 Make the marinade. Mix all the ingredients in a pan. Bring to the boil, then reduce the heat and simmer for 15 minutes. Pour into a non-reactive bowl. Cover and leave to cool.

2 Add the venison cubes and stir to coat. Replace the cover and marinate for 12–48 hours in a cold place, stirring occasionally.

3 Using a slotted spoon, lift out the meat and dry well on kitchen paper. Strain the marinade into a jug (pitcher) and set aside.

4 If using the bacon, cook in a large heavy pan or flameproof casserole over medium heat until the fat runs, then increase the heat and cook for about 4 minutes more, until crisp. Remove from the pan and set aside.

5 Add the butter and oil to the frying pan or casserole and heat until the butter melts. Add the chopped onion and sauté over medium high heat for 4–6 minutes until glazed and golden brown. Using a slotted spoon, transfer the onion to a platter.

6 Add the venison in batches to the fat remaining in the pan and brown over fairly high heat for about 4 minutes to seal. As each batch browns, remove from the pan.

7 When the final batch has browned, return all the venison to the pan, sprinkle with the flour and season with pepper and salt, stirring until the flour has been absorbed. Add the brandy and cook, stirring, for 1 minute more.

8 Add the mushrooms, bouquet garni, onions and bacon (if using). Pour the reserved marinade into the pan and bring to simmering point. Cook over low heat on top of the stove for 1–1½ hours, until meat is very tender.

9 Adjust the seasoning and remove the bouquet garni. Skim the fat from the surface. Stir the cornflour mixture, then add it to the pan, stirring. Cook for 10–15 minutes more, stirring frequently, until the liquid thickens.

10 Serve with poached apples and cranberries, and parsley potatoes.

Meat

All kinds of meat are enjoyed in Belgium, from prime cuts of beef and pork to offal and even horsemeat. These are then transformed into a range of dishes, many of which date back centuries, and all of which showcase the care and thought that typifies Belgian food.

Rich and hearty

Belgium prides itself on the extremely high quality of its meats from various animal breeds. Pork has always been the most important meat, but it wasn't until the 20th century that pork or any other type of meat became commonly consumed on a daily basis by the average citizen.

Before then, most farms or households kept pigs, and these would be slaughtered once or twice a year. These would then serve as the main source of meat protein to nourish the family, and every part of the pig was processed so it could be preserved for the remainder of the year. Standard meat sausages, blood sausages and hams are all still produced around the country, and the meat is the key feature in all manner of dishes, from simple pork chops to delectable roast pork.

Fine quality beef is also highly valued by Belgians, especially in another national dish, *steak frites*, but it is also stewed with beer and served with bread, *frites* or mashed potatoes to make a warming and hearty meal.

The production of beef in Belgium is focused on the famous Belgian Blue Breed, which is recognized for its lean and tender meat, and cows are also farmed to produce top quality veal. Flanders in particular has a worldwide reputation for its calves, which are fed carefully monitored, balanced diets, producing fine-textured, well-flavoured veal.

Certain areas in Belgium are also highly prized for their horsemeat, which is considered a delicacy and dates back to pre-Christian Europe when horsemeat was commonly eaten.

Charcuterie plays an important role in the country's cuisine, and many regional specialities are still produced. These include dried or cured meats such as *filet d'Anvers*, the smoked beef-fillet speciality from Antwerp, and *jambon d'Ardennes*, the flavoursome ham that is hung up in chimneys and slow-smoked over juniper wood. Available at local butchers, these cold cuts are eaten as part of a mixed platter with generous hunks of bread and local cheese and beer.

Serves 4–6

500g/1¼lb stewing beef or
   chuck steak, cubed
20g/¾oz/3 tbsp plain (all-purpose) flour
   for dusting
25g/1oz/2 tbsp butter
30ml/2 tbsp vegetable oil
1 large onion, chopped
2 garlic cloves, crushed
330ml/11½fl oz bottle dark Belgian beer,
   such as Chimay
bouquet garni (see page 70)
30ml/2 tbsp red wine vinegar
30ml/2 tbsp soft light brown sugar
2 slices of rustic bread – white, dark
   brown or spice cake (*peperkoek*)
30ml/2 tbsp Dijon mustard
handful of fresh parsley, chopped
salt and ground black pepper

To serve

fries, potato purée or breads
Belgian Pickles (see page 19)

Flemish-style beef stew with beer
Stoofvlees/Carbonnades à la Flamande

This stew is one of the most famous of all the traditional Flemish dishes. The taste varies from region to region, depending on which type of beer is used to flavour and tenderize the meat. The taste is also influenced by the addition of bread or spice cake, spread with mustard. This is initially placed on top of the stew, but gradually dissolves into it to form a thick sauce.

1 Generously season the beef cubes with salt and pepper, then coat them in the flour.

2 Heat a large, heavy frying pan that has a tight-fitting lid. Melt the butter and the oil over medium to high heat. Add the cubed beef in batches and brown over fairly high heat for about 4 minutes to seal. As each batch browns, remove the cubes from the pan and place them on a plate.

3 Add the onion to the fat remaining in the pan and cook gently for 6–8 minutes, until translucent, then add the garlic and fry for 3 minutes more.

4 Return the meat to the frying pan and stir well to combine with the onions.

5 Pour in the beer and bring the mixture to just below boiling point. Add the bouquet garni, vinegar and brown sugar. Cover the pan, reduce the heat and simmer for 1½ hours or until meat has become tender.

6 Spread the bread thickly with mustard and place it on top of the stew, mustard-side down. Replace the lid and simmer the stew for 20–30 minutes more, stirring occasionally until the meat is very tender. The bread will absorb some of the pan juices and dissolve to thicken the stew.

7 Taste and adjust the seasoning if necessary. Remove the bouquet garni and stir in the parsley. Serve with potato puree, fries or rustic bread, with pickles on the side.

Per portion Energy 317kcal/1324kJ; Protein 21.6g; Carbohydrate 19.8g, of which sugars 8.9g; Fat 15.7g, of which saturates 5.9g; Cholesterol 57mg; Calcium 47mg; Fibre 1.1g; Sodium 314mg.

Steak with fries

Biefstuk met friet/Steak frites

Besides mussels, Belgium's other national dish is *steak frites* – beef steak with French fries. Steak is served in a variety of ways, with all sorts of sauces, but never without fries – the two are inseparable in the national psyche. The best beef in Belgium comes from the White Blue breed of cattle, whose meat is lean and tender, with superior flavour.

1 Heat 40g/1½oz/3 tbsp of the butter and the oil in a large heavy frying pan over high heat. When it is hot, add the steaks and sear them for 1 minute on each side, using tongs to turn them.

2 Reduce the heat to medium and fry the steaks for a further 3–5 minutes on each side, depending on the thickness of the meat and how you like it. Season the steaks on both sides, then transfer them to individual plates. Cover with foil to keep warm.

3 Pour the stock into the frying pan and heat it, stirring and scraping the pan to incorporate the sediment on the base.

4 Add the remaining butter and continue stirring the sauce for 2 minutes. Pour over the steaks and serve immediately, with fries.

Variation

Steak in green peppercorn cream sauce
Fry the steaks in 30ml/2 tbsp clarified butter for 3 minutes on one side until well browned, then turn them over and fry for 3 more minutes (for rare steak) or 4–7 minutes for medium rare. Pour a generous splash of cognac into the pan and set this alight carefully with a long safety match. Shake the pan. When the flames die down, remove the steaks and keep warm. Add to the pan 30ml/2 tbsp drained and rinsed bottled green peppercorns, then whisk in 200ml/7fl oz/scant 1 cup double (heavy) cream. Add a further 30ml/2 tbsp butter and cook over low heat, swirling the pan, until the sauce thickens to coat the back of a spoon. Add 5ml/1 tsp extra cognac to the sauce, season and pour over the steaks. Garnish with watercress and serve with fries.

Serves 4

50g/2oz/¼ cup unsalted (sweet) butter
4 Belgian White Blue beef steaks or
    prime sirloin steaks, each about
    125g/4¼oz, at room temperature
    (see Cook's tip)
15ml/1 tbsp vegetable oil
30ml/2 tbsp beef stock
salt and ground black pepper
Belgian Fries (see page 91), to serve

Cook's tip
Remove the steaks from the refrigerator 1 hour before cooking and let them come to room temperature. This results in juicier meat that will cook evenly.

Per portion Energy 287kcal/1192kJ; Protein 29.5g; Carbohydrate 0.1g, of which sugars 0.1g; Fat 18.7g, of which saturates 9.3g; Cholesterol 90mg; Calcium 9mg; Fibre 0g; Sodium 163mg.

Blind finches with carrots

Blinde vinken or vogeltjes zonder kop met wortelen/Oiseaux sans tête avec des carottes

Serves 4

4 x 90g/3½oz sirloin or flank beef or
   veal steaks
15g/½oz/1 tbsp butter
15ml/1 tbsp oil
2 shallots or 1 small onion, finely chopped
1 garlic clove, finely chopped
500g/1¼lb young carrots, finely chopped
1 bay leaf
2 thyme sprigs
150ml–250ml/5–8fl oz/⅔–1 cup good
   quality Belgian beer
5ml/1 tsp Tierenteyn or Dijon mustard
salt and ground black pepper
chopped fresh parsley, to garnish

For the filling

225g/8oz/1 cup minced (ground) pork
   or a mixture of pork and beef
1 egg yolk
5ml/1 tsp dried sage
2 shallots, finely chopped
15ml/1 tbsp chopped fresh parsley
5ml/1 tsp grated nutmeg
15–45ml/1–3 tbsp breadcrumbs,
   to bind

Per portion Energy 340kcal/1419kJ; Protein 25g;
Carbohydrate 18.2g, of which sugars 12g; Fat 17.9g,
of which saturates 6.4g; Cholesterol 131mg;
Calcium 66mg; Fibre 3.9g; Sodium 450mg.

There are numerous explanations as to how this classic dish got its name. Some say it dates from a period when upper class Belgians regularly dined on finches. Peasants – who could only afford meat once a week on Sundays – could not make the dish, so they invented their own version, using veal and minced beef or pork. They called it "blind finches" because, although the pieces of meat were vaguely bird-shaped, they had no eyes. Ready-to-cook Blind Finches are on sale in most Belgian butcher's shops, but it is fun and easy to make your own at home.

1 Put all the ingredients for the filling in a large bowl, using just enough of the breadcrumbs to bind the mixture. Mix well. Cool and dampen hands by running them under cold water, then roll the filling into 4 oval shapes of equal size. Set aside.

2 Put each steak between two sheets of clear film (plastic wrap) and pound it with a meat mallet or rolling pin until it is 5mm/¼in thick and large enough to wrap a portion of filling. Fold the steak over the filling and tuck in the ends in to make a parcel. Tie with kitchen string (twine) to maintain the shape.

3 Melt the butter in the oil in a large, heavy frying pan over medium heat. When it is hot, but not smoking, add the meat rolls and cook for about 10 minutes, turning occasionally until browned on all sides. Using tongs, transfer the rolls to a plate and cover with foil to keep warm.

4 Add the shallots or onion to the fat remaining in the pan and sauté for about 5 minutes to soften but not brown.

5 Stir in the garlic, carrots, bay leaf and thyme, then return the beef rolls to the pan, season well and pour in the beer. Bring to the boil, then reduce the heat, cover and simmer for 10 minutes.

6 Turn the beef rolls over, stir the mustard into the vegetables, replace the lid and simmer for 8–10 minutes more or until the carrots are tender and the meat rolls and their filling are cooked through.

7 Remove the string from the beef rolls and divide among warmed plates.

8 Remove the whole herbs from the carrot mixture, then spoon it on to the plates. Sprinkle with chopped parsley and serve.

Birds' nests with pink potato purée
Vogel nestjes/Nid d'oiseaux

Serves 4

4 eggs
225g/8oz/1 cup minced (ground) beef
225g/8oz/1 cup minced (ground) pork
1 shallot, finely chopped
a pinch each of grated nutmeg
    and dried thyme
45ml/3 tbsp chopped fresh parsley
1 egg, beaten
egg white and fresh white breadcrumbs,
    for coating
15g/½oz/1 tbsp butter
15ml/1 tbsp vegetable oil or olive oil
chopped fresh parsley, to serve

For the tomato sauce

4 large tomatoes or 400g/14oz can
    chopped tomatoes
15g/½oz/1 tbsp butter
15ml/1 tbsp vegetable oil or olive oil
2–3 shallots or 1 small onion, chopped
1 garlic clove, finely chopped
30ml/2 tbsp tomato purée (paste)
30ml/2 tbsp sherry or Madeira
1 bay leaf
5ml/1 tsp paprika
salt and ground black pepper

For the potato purée

500g/1¼lb potatoes, peeled
500ml/17fl oz/generous 2 cups milk
    or cream
40g/1½oz/3 tbsp unsalted (sweet) butter
30ml/2 tbsp tomato purée
pinch of grated nutmeg

Cook's tip

To peel the tomatoes, remove the stems, then cut a cross on the bottom of each of them. Add to a pan of boiling water. After 30 seconds or so, the skin will begin to peel back from the crosses. Lift the tomatoes out with a slotted spoon, place them in cold water to prevent them from cooking further, then peel off the skins.

Per portion Energy 734kcal/3067kJ; Protein 39.1g; Carbohydrate 41g, of which sugars 13.1g; Fat 46.5g, of which saturates 20.5g; Cholesterol 359mg; Calcium 234mg; Fibre 2.9g; Sodium 406mg.

This traditional Belgian Easter treat resembles the British dish called Scotch eggs. It originated in medieval times as a way of preserving the eggs that were denied to Catholics during the Lenten fast. When the eggs are cut in half, they look like birds' nests. Children love them, especially when they are served with tomato sauce and pink potato purée.

1 Put the eggs in a pan with water to cover. Bring to the boil, reduce the heat slightly and cook for 10 minutes. Drain and cool quickly in iced water. As soon as the eggs are cold, shell them and set them aside.

2 Put the beef and pork in a bowl. Add the shallot, nutmeg, thyme, parsley and egg. Mix with clean hands until it holds together.

3 Divide the meat mixture into 4 portions and knead each one around a hard-boiled egg to make an even coating 2cm/¾in thick. Put the egg white and breadcrumbs in separate shallow dishes. Dip each covered egg in egg white, then roll in breadcrumbs until evenly coated.

4 Melt the butter in the oil in a large frying pan over medium heat. Add the covered eggs and brown them on all sides. Reduce the heat, cover and cook for 30 minutes.

5 Meanwhile, make the sauce. If using fresh tomatoes, skin them (see cook's tip) and process in a blender or food processor.

6 In a pan, melt the butter in the oil. Add the shallots or onion and sauté for 3 minutes, then add the garlic and sauté for 3 minutes more. Add the processed or canned tomatoes, then stir in the tomato purée. Simmer for 5 minutes, then add the sherry or Madeira and the bay leaf. Season and add the paprika. Cook over low heat for 20 minutes.

7 Meanwhile, make the potato purée. Put the potatoes in a pan with lightly salted water to cover. Bring to the boil, reduce the heat and simmer for about 25 minutes until just tender. Drain the potatoes, return them to the pan and place over the heat to dry. Mash with the milk or cream, butter, tomato purée and nutmeg to make a smooth paste.

8 Pile the potato purée in the centre of 4 warm plates. Surround with most of the sauce. Cut the meatballs in half so the eggs are visible and arrange 2 halves on the sauce on each of the plates. Spoon the remaining sauce over, but make sure the egg yolks are still visible. Garnish with the parsley and serve.

Pork chops in mustard sauce

Varkens koteletten met mosterd saus/Côtelettes de porc à la moutarde

Ever since the days when every rural family kept a pig, pork has been a favourite meat in Belgium and there are many pork dishes in the culinary repertoire. Many of these recipes, such as this one, include mustard, which is also a popular accompaniment for cheeses and cold meats. The tradition of fine mustard-making was established in Belgium in the 13th century, and continues to the present day.

1 Season the pork chops generously with salt and pepper. Heat a heavy frying pan over medium to high heat. Add the butter and oil and swirl to coat. Add the chops and fry them for 4 minutes on each side or until cooked to your taste. Using tongs, transfer the chops to a platter, cover and keep warm.

2 Reheat the fat remaining in the frying pan and sauté the shallots for 3–5 minutes, stirring frequently, until softened.

3 Add the wine or beer. Cook, stirring well to incorporate the sediment on the base of the pan, for about 2 minutes, then whisk in the cream and mustard and bring to the boil. Reduce the heat and simmer the sauce for about 3 minutes, until it is slightly thickened. Season to taste.

4 Pour the sauce over the pork chops. Garnish with parsley and serve with the beans, Brussels sprouts and potatoes.

Serves 4

4 pork loin chops, about 2.5cm/1in thick
25g/1oz/2 tbsp unsalted (sweet) butter
5ml/1 tsp vegetable oil or olive oil
4 shallots, chopped
200ml/7fl oz/scant 1 cup white wine or
   Belgian blond beer
200ml/7fl oz/scant 1 cup double
   (heavy) cream
30ml/2 tbsp good-quality mustard
salt and ground black pepper
30ml/2 tbsp chopped fresh parsley,
   to garnish
green beans, Brussels sprouts and boiled
   potatoes, to serve

Cook's tip

Pork chops can easily be overcooked and become dry. Thinner cuts will take less time and can be cooked at a higher heat. For thicker cuts, reduce the heat and increase the cooking time.

Per portion Energy 551kcal/2285kJ; Protein 33.7g; Carbohydrate 3.1g, of which sugars 2.6g; Fat 41.4g, of which saturates 22.4g; Cholesterol 176mg; Calcium 50mg; Fibre 0.2g; Sodium 378mg.

Serves 4

25g/1oz/2 tbsp butter

2 onions, halved and thinly sliced

500g/1¼lb cooking apples, peeled, cored, halved and sliced

a pinch each of sugar, ground cinnamon and grated nutmeg

4 medium blood sausages

salt and ground black pepper

mustard, Belgian Pickles (see page 19) and dark rye bread, to serve

Per portion Energy 340kcal/1420kJ; Protein 9g; Carbohydrate 29.5g, of which sugars 15.5g; Fat 21.6g, of which saturates 9.6g; Cholesterol 64mg; Calcium 115mg; Fibre 3.2g; Sodium 748mg.

Blood sausage with onions

Bloedworst met ajuin en appelen/Boudin noir avec des oignons et des pommes

Blood sausages, also called *bloed worst*, *zwarte pens*, *beuling* or *boudin noir*, date back to the 14th century. Like the British speciality, black pudding, they are made by mixing the blood from freshly slaughtered pigs with spices, cereal, salt and sometimes onions. The delicacy is very popular in Belgium, especially as a winter dish, when blood sausages are traditionally served with mustard or pickles, dark rye bread and baked apples.

1 Melt the butter in a large frying pan that has a lid. Add the onions and cook over medium heat for 8–12 minutes, until they start to soften.

2 Add the apple slices to the pan, then sprinkle with the sugar to promote caramelization, and sauté for 5 minutes more, stirring frequently.

3 Add the cinnamon and grate the nutmeg into the pan. Season with salt and pepper.

4 Add the sausages to the pan, cover and cook for 10 minutes, stirring occasionally to prevent the apples from sticking to the pan.

5 Remove the lid and turn the sausages over, using tongs to avoid puncturing them. Give the apples a stir, cover the pan again and cook for 5 minutes more or until the sausages are well done.

6 Serve immediately with the mustard or pickles and a few slices of dark rye bread.

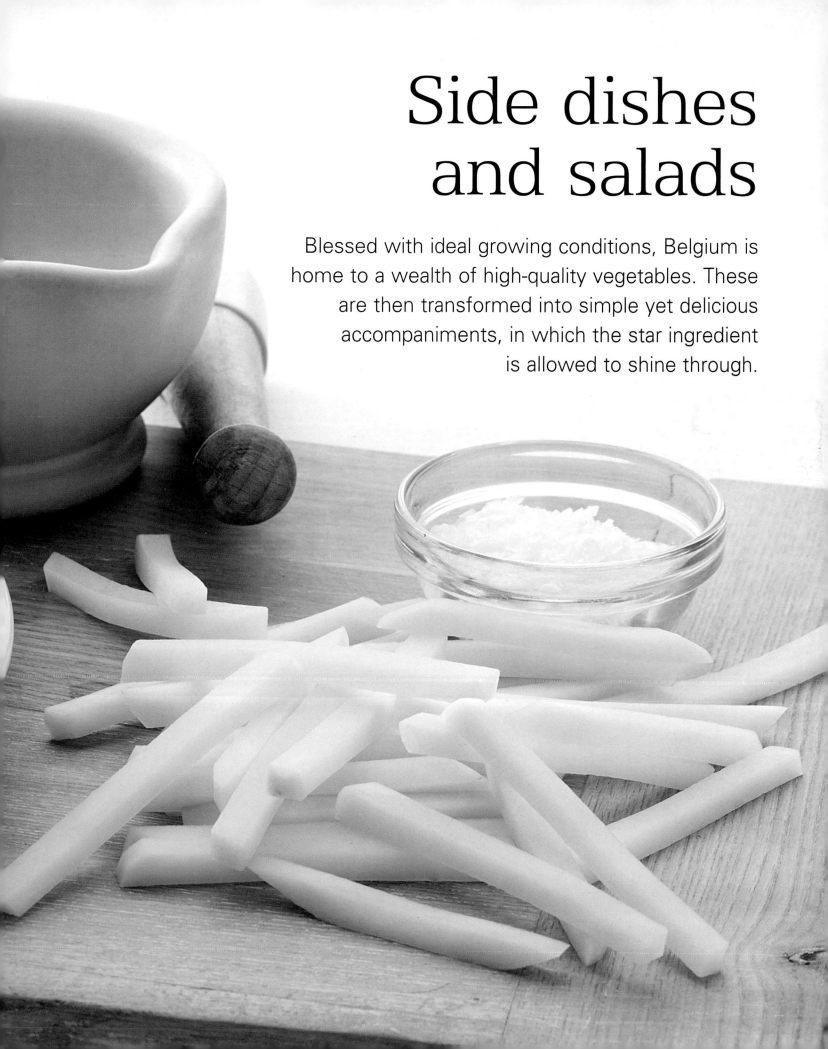

Side dishes and salads

Blessed with ideal growing conditions, Belgium is home to a wealth of high-quality vegetables. These are then transformed into simple yet delicious accompaniments, in which the star ingredient is allowed to shine through.

Light and fresh

With an enviable range of seasonal vegetables to choose from, it is little wonder that Belgium has a considerable and diverse list of vegetable dishes as part of its culinary repertoire. These are often prepared and served simply as an accompaniment to a main course, or enjoyed as appetizers and soups.

Following the introduction of the potato from the New World around 1600, Belgium quickly started cultivating it widely. It soon became a staple food, and Belgium remains a nation of fervent potato-eaters. This love affair is reflected by the tuber's appearance in many old Flemish proverbs, including the commonly used phrase "tussen the soep en de patatten " ("between the soup and the potatoes"), which denotes a small window of time between two tasks when something can be achieved.

Potatoes remain well represented in Belgium's daily diet, and vegetable markets and supermarkets provide a multitude of the finest and best-quality varieties of potato available, including Bintje, said to be the best type of potato for making the nation's beloved *frites*.

Cruciferous vegetables are indispensable as winter side dishes, tasting best after the first frost has arrived, and ranging from green to red cabbages, to cauliflowers and Brussels sprouts. They might be mixed into heartwarming *stoemps* or an earthy "hotchpotch", or simply served as a garnish or side dish to accompany meat dishes.

Vegetables grown exclusively in Belgium, such as salsify, *witloof* or endives, white asparagus and hop shoots, are highly sought after by connoisseurs during the brief seasons while they are at their peak.

Vegetables are not the only ingredients used as accompaniments to main courses. Fresh and dried fruits, such as cherries, apples, prunes and berries are often used to make aromatic side dishes that perfectly complement game and roasts. Many of these are based on medieval cooking methods using infusions of spices, mustards, beer or spirits.

Red cabbage braised with apples

Rode kool met appeltjes/Chou rouge
aux pommes

Red cabbage is a traditional vegetable whose use is profoundly ingrained in Belgian cuisine. The Flemish predilection for mixing sweet and sour flavours and combining vegetables with fruits and spices takes this classic dish into another dimension. The flavours are complex and earthy, making it a great companion for hearty meat, game or sausage dishes.

1 Heat the butter or oil in a heavy flameproof casserole or pan. Add the onion and sauté, stirring frequently, for 5 minutes, or until lightly browned.

2 Add the cabbage and stir thoroughly to coat in the fat. Immediately pour in the vinegar. Add the apples and cook for 3 minutes more, stirring frequently.

3 Roll each clove in a bay leaf and push down inside the casserole. Bring to the boil, then reduce the heat to low. Cover and simmer for 1½–2 hours, stirring occasionally, or until the cabbage is tender.

4 Check the casserole from time to time to make sure that the cabbage remains moist. If it seems dry, add a tablespoon of boiling water. When the cabbage is done, there should be hardly any liquid left in the bottom of the casserole.

5 Season with salt and pepper, then add the cinnamon, with brown sugar to taste. This dish should have a nice sweet and sour balance. Simmer for 3 minutes more, until the sugar has dissolved completely.

6 Remove the bay leaves and cloves, tip the cabbage into a heated bowl and serve.

Serves 4

65g/2½oz/5 tbsp butter or 75ml/5 tbsp oil
1 onion, finely chopped
675g/1½lb red cabbage, evenly shredded
   (see Cook's tips)
90–120ml/6–8 tbsp white or red
   wine vinegar
3–4 cooking apples, peeled and sliced
2 cloves
2 fresh bay leaves
salt and ground black pepper
pinch of ground cinnamon
15–30ml/1–2 tbsp soft dark brown sugar

Cook's tips

• To prepare the cabbage, first remove any damaged outer leaves. Slice the cabbage in half lengthways. Cut a V-shaped wedge around the white core and remove it. Slice both pieces in half again, then slice or shred the cabbage with a sharp cook's knife.
• Adjust the amount of vinegar or sugar, depending on how tart the apples are.

Per portion Energy 222kcal/924kJ; Protein 3g; Carbohydrate 22.6g, of which sugars 22g; Fat 13.8g, of which saturates 8.5g; Cholesterol 35mg; Calcium 95mg; Fibre 5.4g; Sodium 113mg.

Serves 4

2 firm, sharp, eating apples
45ml/3 tbsp sugar
500ml/17fl oz/generous 2 cups water
juice of ½ lemon

For the berry compote

250/9oz/2½ cups cranberries
60–90ml/4–6 tbsp water
150g/5oz/¾ cup sugar, or to taste
5–10ml/1–2 tsp lemon juice

Per portion Energy 250kcal/1069kJ; Protein 0.8g; Carbohydrate 65.6g, of which sugars 65.6g; Fat 0.2g, of which saturates 0g; Cholesterol 0mg; Calcium 33mg; Fibre 2.7g; Sodium 6mg.

Poached apples with berry compote
Gestoofde appelen met veenbessen compote/Pommes à la compote d'airelles

The small trailing cranberries that grow in Belgium, known locally as either *veenbessen* or *airelles*, are paler than their more robust American cousins and have a slightly different flavour. These jewel-like fruit are often partnered with poached apples or pears. In the Ardennes area, the combination is regularly served with poultry and game, especially wild boar.

1 Peel the apples and cut them in half. Cut away the stem and core from each with a paring knife and use a spoon to enlarge the core space and create a cavity.

2 In a pan large enough to hold the apple halves in a single layer, heat the sugar with the water. Bring to the boil, stirring occasionally to make a syrup.

3 Stir in the lemon juice. Reduce the heat and place the apple halves in the pan, so they are covered with syrup. Cover and simmer for about 20 minutes or until they are tender but still hold their shape.

4 Lift out the apples with a slotted spoon and drain on a wire rack over a baking sheet.

5 Make the berry compote. Rinse the berries and put them in a pan with the water. Add the sugar and bring to the boil. Reduce the heat, cover and simmer for 10 minutes or until the berries have softened. Stir occasionally and skim off any foam that rises to the surface.

6 Add 5ml/1 tsp of the lemon juice, taste and adjust for sweetness. If necessary, add more sugar, heating until it dissolves.

7 Transfer the apples to a platter, with the cavities uppermost. Fill them with the berry compote. To serve warm, reheat the apples in a shallow pan for about 5 minutes. They can also be served chilled. Offer any remaining berry compote in a separate bowl.

Peas and carrots Flemish style

Erwtjes en worteltjes op vlaamse wijze/Petit pois
et des carottes à la Flamande

From the middle of May until mid-July, Belgians indulge in one of their favourite treats: fresh peas. Sweet and tender, they are delicious eaten raw, or can be accompanied by young carrots, pearl onions, garden lettuce and salty bacon or cured ham. This dish is especially popular served with roast pork or beef for the traditional Belgian Sunday meal.

1 Bring a pan of salted water to the boil. Add the carrots and cook for 3 minutes. Remove with a slotted spoon and leave to dry.

2 Pod the peas and add them to the pan of boiling water. Cook for 2 minutes, then drain and add the peas to a bowl of iced water to stop them from cooking any further. Drain and set aside.

3 Melt 25g/1oz/2 tbsp of the butter in a large frying pan. Add the bacon and sauté for 3 minutes, then add the onions and sauté for 4 minutes. When the onions are translucent, add the carrots and sauté for 3 minutes until they are glazed.

4 Pour in the stock, cover and cook for 10–15 minutes, or until all the liquid has been absorbed. Add the lettuce and cook for 3–5 minutes until the strips have wilted.

5 Add the peas, with the remaining butter. Simmer for 2–3 minutes until the peas are just tender. Add the sugar and nutmeg, season and stir to mix. Spoon into a warmed bowl, garnish with parsley and serve.

Variation

If available, substitute smoked ham from the Ardennes or Ganda for the bacon, or use Breydel ham from Flanders. Sauté for just 1 minute, not 3.

Serves 4–6

8 young carrots, thinly sliced
1.6kg/3½lb fresh peas in pods or
   575g/1¼lb/5 cups frozen peas
40g/1½oz/3 tbsp butter
115g/4oz rindless smoked bacon,
   cut into fine strips
100g/3¾oz/⅔ cup baby or small pearl
   onions, peeled and left whole
100ml/3½fl oz/scant ½ cup chicken stock
1 small lettuce, cut in thin strips
pinch of sugar and grated nutmeg
salt and ground black pepper
chopped fresh parsley, to garnish

Cook's tip

Shell the peas just before cooking them. Pinch off the stem, then pull the string down the full length of the pod. The pod will pop open so the peas can be removed.

Per portion Energy 141kcal/585kJ; Protein 9.8g; Carbohydrate 15.5g, of which sugars 7.4g; Fat 4.9g, of which saturates 1.5g; Cholesterol 10mg; Calcium 49mg; Fibre 5.8g; Sodium 311mg.

Belgian fries
Frieten/Pommes Frites

Every village or town in Belgium has *friterie* or *fritkot* stands selling fries in tight paper cones, served with a variety of condiments, including mayonnaise and Belgian pickles. The key to these crisp, tasty and grease-free fries is the use of a specific type of potato – Bintje – and a cooking method that involves double frying in clean oil or suet.

1 Line a baking sheet with kitchen paper. Peel the potatoes, cut them in 1cm/½in thick slices, then stack the slices and cut them in 1cm/½in batons. Place in a bowl of cold water to remove some of the starch and to keep them from turning brown.

2 Half fill a heavy pan with oil. If using a deep-fryer, fill it to the level recommended in the instruction book. Heat the oil to 160°C/325°F or until a cube of bread, added to the oil, turns golden in about 45 seconds.

3 While the oil is heating, drain the potatoes and dry them in a clean cloth. This will prevent the oil from spitting when they are added.

4 Add the potatoes, in small batches, to the frying basket. Fry for 4–8 minutes, depending on the thickness and variety, shaking the pan occasionally. After this preliminary cooking, the fries should be cooked through but not yet golden. Lift them out, shake off the excess oil, then spread them on the paper-lined baking sheet. Leave to cool slightly.

5 Reheat the oil, this time to 180°C/350°F. Return the par-cooked potatoes to the oil in small batches and fry for 4 minutes until golden and crisp. Drain on fresh kitchen paper, season with salt and serve with mayonnaise or pickles.

Serves 4–6

1 kg/2¼ lb maincrop potatoes
  (see Cook's tips)
peanut or other vegetable oil, for frying
salt
Mayonnaise (see page 20) and/or Belgian
  Pickles (see page 19), to serve

Cook's tips
• Potatoes that are suitable for making chips or fries vary from country to country, so ask your supplier. In Belgium, the best variety is said to be Bintje, while English cooks swear by Maris Piper, King Edward or Sante. In America, Russet Burbank potatoes are widely used for fries.
• Cut the potatoes by hand or use a chip cutter so that they are of uniform thickness.
• Don't cut the potatoes too thinly or they will absorb a lot of fat and have less flavour.
• Don't fry too many potatoes at one time or the temperature of the fat will drop.

Per portion Energy 467kcal/1957kJ; Protein 5.5g; Carbohydrate 56.7g, of which sugars 2.2g; Fat 18.3g, of which saturates 9.7g; Cholesterol 0mg; Calcium 23mg; Fibre 3.6g; Sodium 517mg.

Potato, bean and bacon salad

Luikse salade/Salade Liégeoise

This specialty salad comes from Liège, the French-speaking centre of Wallonia. From mid May until the end of October, crisp garden green beans are at their peak. They partner potatoes in this classic salad, which is a popular menu item at restaurants and brasseries. It makes a satisfying lunch and is usually accompanied with a refreshing Belgian local beer.

1 Put the potatoes in a large pan with lightly salted water to cover. Bring to the boil and cook for 15–20 minutes.

2 Meanwhile, cook the beans in a separate pan of lightly salted water for 5 minutes.

3 Drain in a colander, rinse with cold water to prevent further cooking, then pat dry with kitchen paper. Put the beans in a salad bowl and cover with foil to keep warm.

4 Heat the oil in a frying pan and fry the bacon over medium heat for 7 minutes, or until crisp. Remove the bacon with a slotted spoon and scatter it over the beans. Cover again. Set the frying pan aside.

5 When the potatoes are tender, but still fairly firm, drain them. When they are cool enough to handle, cut into slices or quarters.

6 Return the frying pan to the heat. When the bacon fat is hot, add the onion and fry for 8–10 minutes until golden brown. Tip the contents of the pan over the beans and bacon, then add the potatoes. Mix gently.

7 Pour the wine vinegar into the frying pan. Boil rapidly for 2 minutes, stirring constantly to incorporate any bits of bacon or onion that have stuck to the base. Pour the mixture over the salad. Season and toss to coat. Sprinkle with chopped parsley and serve immediately, while still warm.

Serves 4

600g/1lb 6oz potatoes, scrubbed
   but not peeled
500g/1¼lb/3½–4 cups fine green
   beans, trimmed
15ml/1 tbsp vegetable oil
150g/5oz smoked bacon, finely chopped
1 small onion, finely chopped
90ml/6 tbsp red wine vinegar
salt and ground black pepper
15ml/1 tbsp chopped fresh parsley,
   to garnish

Per portion Energy 246kcal/1029kJ; Protein 11.3g; Carbohydrate 29.3g, of which sugars 5.7g; Fat 10.1g, of which saturates 2.9g; Cholesterol 20mg; Calcium 60mg; Fibre 4.5g; Sodium 595mg.

Serves 4

4 ripe but firm tomatoes on the vine
2–3 shallots, finely chopped
45ml/3 tbsp chopped fresh parsley
    or dill
30ml/2 tbsp red wine vinegar
90ml/6 tbsp vegetable oil, olive oil
    or a mixture
salt and ground black pepper

Cook's tip
The fresher the tomatoes, the better this
salad will be. They should be full-flavoured
and firm enough to slice neatly with a
serrated knife. If you like, you can peel the
tomatoes before slicing them, but this is
not strictly necessary.

Per portion Energy 171kcal/705kJ; Protein 1.1g;
Carbohydrate 3.9g, of which sugars 3.5g; Fat 16.9g,
of which saturates 2g; Cholesterol 0mg; Calcium
34mg; Fibre 1.6g; Sodium 11mg.

Classic tomato salad
Tomaten salade/Salade de tomate

Tomatoes are an important crop in Belgium. During the summer months
Flemish greenhouses and fields are filled with tomatoes that differ widely
in size, quality and texture and every year new varieties become available
to meet an increasing demand. Home cooks and restaurateurs alike
heighten their summer menus with this classic and colourful tomato salad.

1 Remove the stem and core from each
tomato, then slice them evenly and arrange
them on a serving platter.

2 Sprinkle with the shallots, season with
salt and pepper and sprinkle with the
chopped parsley or dill.

3 Make a simple dressing by putting the
vinegar in a bowl and whisking in the oil.
Drizzle the dressing over the tomatoes.

4 Cover with clear film (plastic wrap)
and marinate for 30 minutes at room
temperature before serving.

Variation
The herbs can be varied, depending on
what you have in the garden. Tarragon is a
good addition, especially if the salad is to
be served with fish. Strip the leaves from
a sprig of tarragon and chop them finely
before scattering them over the salad.

Desserts and drinks

Belgians love fine foods, and this is nowhere more apparent than in their beautifully crafted desserts, confections and drinks. From simple fruit-based desserts and rich chocolate treats, to refined coffees and piquant liqueurs, there is always something tempting on offer at the end of a meal.

Sweet and creamy

Belgium is a nation of *bon vivants*, a trait that is not only expressed in their love of fine food rituals but also in their drinking habits. This devotion to top quality produce is especially manifest in its world-famous chocolate industry as well as its glorious patisseries, which are stocked daily with an overwhelming assortment of fabulous pastries, candies and fine desserts created by highly trained and skilled Belgian patissiers. From delicate and complex chocolate creations, such as truffles and pralines, to fruit-based desserts or cheese and rice puddings, the range of foods on offer will satisfy even the sweetest tooth.

Among the many delectable desserts are those made by soaking or cooking fruit in wine or beer, a tradition that dates back to medieval times. The plump, flavoursome fruits are then coupled with creamy rice pudding or rich cheesecake, elevating the dishes to new heights. Chocolate desserts, such as ice cream sundae with chocolate sauce or chocolate mousse are also a common sight on the Belgian menu.

As with most chocolate recipes, it is important that you use a good quality product with a high cocoa content in order to achieve the desired richness and complexity of flavour.

Belgians enjoy a drink with their meal, and take care to choose an appropriate one for each course. In addition to the 500 varieties of beer available, Belgium also produces wine and excellent distilled spirits or liqueurs, which marry well with its food.

Every region or province produces some kind of liqueur, infused with fruits or juniper berries, herbs or secret spice concoctions that date back several centuries and are eagerly promoted to the consumer as being a good cure for all kinds of ailments.

According to Belgian tradition, an enjoyable meal should be accompanied with appropriate drinks: an aperitif to commence to promote a good appetite; a well-matched wine with dinner; and a stimulating coffee with a shot of liqueur or spirit to mark the perfect end to a meal that will satisfy both heart and soul.

Rice porridge with braised prunes

Rijstpap met gestoofde pruimen/Riz au lait et pruneaux

Rice porridge – or *rijstpap* as it is known in Belgium – is thought to have originated in the 16th century, when Emperor Charles V's soldiers returned from fighting the Ottoman Empire, bringing with them rice and exotic spices like cinnamon and saffron. Spices, especially saffron, were very expensive, so their use indicated the host's wealth and generosity. The prunes hark back to medieval times, when fresh fruits were not available in winter.

1 Start by preparing the prunes. Drain them and put them in a pan with the lemon rind, beer, cinnamon stick and sugar. Simmer, uncovered, for 30 minutes or until they are soft and tender and the cooking liquid is very syrupy.

2 Meanwhile, put the rice in a colander and rinse under cold water. Rinse a heavy pan in cold water, tip out the excess but do not dry the pan as this will help to stop the rice from sticking.

3 Add the milk, rice, cinnamon stick, saffron and salt to the pan, with the vanilla pod, if using. Bring to the boil, reduce the heat, cover and simmer for 30 minutes, stirring occasionally with a wooden spoon.

4 When the rice is tender, but still retains some "bite", stir in the sugar. If using vanilla extract or vanilla sugar instead of the split bean, stir it in to the mixture. Simmer for 5 minutes more.

5 When all the milk has been absorbed and the *rijstpap* is thick and creamy, remove the cinnamon stick and vanilla bean (if using). Spoon into dessert bowls and top each portion with 15–30ml/1–2 tbsp of the prunes. Serve warm or cold.

Variations

For a simpler version of *rijstpap*, simply top each portion with soft light brown sugar. The beer-braised prunes can also be served as a side dish with meat or game.

Serves 4–6

150g/5oz/⅔ cup medium grain rice, such as paella rice
1 litre/1¾ pints/4 cups full cream (whole) milk
1 cinnamon stick
pinch of crushed saffron threads
pinch of salt
1 vanilla pod (bean), split, or 5ml/1 tsp pure vanilla extract, or 1 x 8g/⅓oz sachet vanilla sugar
75g/3oz/6 tbsp sugar

For the prunes

400g/14oz/1¾ cups dried prunes, soaked in water for 3–4 hours
strip of pared unwaxed lemon rind
400ml/14fl oz/1⅔ cups dark abbey beer, such as Chimay or Leffe
1 cinnamon stick
75g/3oz/scant ½ cup soft light brown sugar

Cook's tip

It is important to use full cream milk; the fat content stops the rice from burning.

Per portion Energy 412kcal/1734kJ; Protein 9.4g; Carbohydrate 76.2g, of which sugars 56.3g; Fat 6.9g, of which saturates 4.2g; Cholesterol 23mg; Calcium 241mg; Fibre 3.8g; Sodium 85mg.

Serves 4

2 firm ripe cooking pears
500ml/17fl oz/generous 2 cups red wine
100g/3½oz/½ cup sugar
pared rind of 1 orange
2 whole cloves
1 cinnamon stick
1 peppercorn
ice cream or whipped cream, to serve
4 mint leaves, to decorate

Cook's tip

Use a skewer to check that the pears are cooked. They should be soft enough that the skewer slides in, but not so soft that they are in danger of breaking up. The cooking time required will depend on the variety of pear used, and the ripeness.

Per portion Energy 378kcal/1595kJ; Protein 1g; Carbohydrate 85.7g, of which sugars 85.7g; Fat 0.2g, of which saturates 0g; Cholesterol 0mg; Calcium 53mg; Fibre 3.9g; Sodium 22mg.

Poached pears in spiced red wine

Gestoofde peertjes in rode wijn/Poires pochées au vin rouge

Until the 16th century, pears were used only for cooking in Europe. Poached pears, like the ones in this recipe, were often sold by street vendors. A popular expression, warning that an apparently profitable situation may have unexpected consequences, recalls this period with the words: "met de gebakken peren blijven zitten" ("getting stuck with unsold cooked pears").

1 Peel the pears, cut them in half and scoop out the cores to leave a neat, round cavity in each. Put the pear halves in a shallow pan and pour over the wine to cover them completely. Sprinkle with the sugar.

2 Pierce the strip of orange rind with the cloves. Add to the pan with the cinnamon stick and peppercorn. Bring to the boil, then reduce the heat, cover the pan and simmer for 30–45 minutes (see Cook's tip).

3 Using a slotted spoon, lift the pears out and place them on a serving platter or in individual bowls. Increase the heat under the pan and boil the wine mixture for about 10 minutes until it has reduced by half and become syrupy.

4 Lift out and discard the orange rind, cinnamon stick and peppercorn. Spoon the syrup over the pears and leave to cool.

5 Serve at room temperature or chill until required, periodically basting the pears with the syrup so they develop a warm glossy red hue.

6 Trim the base of each pear half if necessary so that it lies flat, with the cavity uppermost. Fill the cavities with ice cream or whipped cream, decorate with the mint leaves and serve immediately.

Variation

To enrich the syrup, whisk in 15ml/1 tbsp brandy before spooning it over the pears.

Cheesecake with sour cherries

Plattekaas taart met krieken/Tarte au fromage et cerises

Serves 6–8

500g/1¼lb jar stoned (pitted) Morello
   cherries in syrup

60m/4 tbsp water

30ml/2 tbsp powdered gelatine

150ml/¼ pint/⅔ cup Kriek beer, such as
   St. Louis, Belle-Vue or Lindemans

500g/1¼lb/2¼ cups Quark, soft cheese or
   fromage frais

150ml/¼ pint/⅔ cup crème fraîche or
   sour cream

200ml/7fl oz/scant 1 cup double
   (heavy) cream

115g/4oz/generous ½ cup caster
   (superfine) sugar

90ml/6 tbsp flaked (sliced) almonds,
   to decorate (optional)

For the crust

200g/7oz *speculaas* cookies (spice
   cookies) or other cookies suitable
   for crumbing

100g/3½oz/scant ½ cup unsalted
   (sweet) butter

30ml/2 tbsp cherry jam (optional)

Cook's tip

To remove the cheesecake from the tin,
rinse a slim metal spatula or knife with
very hot water, dry quickly and run the
spatula between the cheesecake and
the sides of the tin. Unclip the spring
and lift off the sides of the tin. Run the
spatula under the cheesecake to loosen
it from the base and transfer it carefully
to a serving platter.

Per portion Energy 574kcal/2394kJ; Protein 6.5g;
Carbohydrate 50.1g, of which sugars 39g; Fat 39.5g,
of which saturates 24.9g; Cholesterol 87mg;
Calcium 145mg; Fibre 0.7g; Sodium 198mg.

Belgians love sour or Morello cherries. The fruit features in sauces, poultry
and game dishes and meat stews, as well as in desserts like this chilled
no-bake cheesecake. The base is traditionally made using Belgium's
favourite cookie – *speculaas* – while the creamy cheese topping is studded
with cherries and spiked with some of the cherry-flavoured Kriek beer for
which the country is famous. Serve it with a glass of Kriek too, if you like.

1 Make the crust. Crumb the cookies in a
food processor or put them between sheets
of baking parchment and crush with a rolling
pin. Tip into a bowl.

2 Melt the butter in a pan and stir it into
the crumbs with the jam, if using. Mix well.
Using clean hands, shape into a ball.

3 Place in a 23cm/9in springform cake tin
(pan) and press out to form an even base.
Cover with plastic wrap (clear film) and place
in the refrigerator.

4 Drain the cherries in a colander, reserving
the syrup in a measuring jug (cup). Chop
115g/4oz/⅔ cup of the cherries and set
them aside. Leave the remaining cherries
in the colander.

5 Put the water in a cup and sprinkle the
gelatine on the surface. Leave until spongy.

6 Pour 150ml/¼ pint/⅔ cup of the syrup
from the cherries into a pan. Bring to the
boil, then cool for 30 seconds.

7 Whisk in the gelatine until dissolved. Stir
in the Kriek beer and strain the mixture into
a jug (pitcher).

8 In a large bowl, beat the Quark, soft
cheese or fromage frais with the crème
fraîche or sour cream, and gradually add
the gelatine mixture. Fold in the reserved
chopped cherries.

9 Whip the cream with the sugar in a bowl,
until stiff peaks form. Carefully fold it into
the cheese mixture.

10 Spoon the filling over the crumb base
in the pan and smooth the top with a wetted
spoon or spatula. Cover with clear film
(plastic wrap). Chill in the refrigerator for
at least 4 hours or overnight.

11 Remove the cheesecake from the tin
(see Cook's tip) and transfer it to a serving
platter. Sprinkle the flaked almonds over the
surface of the cheesecake and press some
on to the sides. Serve in slices, with the
drained cherries.

Serves 4–6

500g/1¼lb/5–6 cups strawberries
100g/3½oz/scant 1 cup icing
    (confectioners') sugar
400ml/14fl oz/1⅔ cups double
    (heavy) cream
25g/1oz/¼ cup almond slivers

Cook's tip
For best results, use freshly picked
strawberries. Rinse them lightly before
hulling, if necessary, but do not soak in
water or they will become soggy and
the flavour will be spoiled. Pat dry with
kitchen paper.

Strawberry mousse, Waasland-style

Aardbeienschuim op Waaslandse wijze/Mousse de
fraises a la manière de Waasland

Several areas in Belgium produce succulent strawberries. One such region
is Waasland, which since 1953 has held an annual festival in Melsele. This
is based on a 16th-century tradition, in which the first fruits of the year
were offered to the Virgin Mary in the Chapel of Gaverland. The modern
festivities include the election of Miss Strawberry, who has the honour of
offering the first of the new season's crop to the Belgian King and Queen.

1 Cut half of the strawberries into quarters.
Place them in a single layer in a decorative
glass bowl. Sprinkle half of the icing sugar
on top.

2 In a food processor or blender, purée the
remaining strawberries with half of the cream.
Add 30–60ml/2–4 tbsp of the remaining
icing sugar, depending upon the sweetness
of the strawberries, and process until
smooth. Pour over the cut strawberries
in the bowl.

3 Toast the almonds over medium heat in
a dry, heavy frying pan until golden brown,
shaking the pan often to prevent them from
burning. Leave to cool.

4 Beat the remaining cream with enough
of the remaining icing sugar to sweeten it.
Spread or pipe the cream over the purée.

5 Sprinkle the toasted almonds on top,
cover with clear film (plastic wrap) and place
in the refrigerator until ready to serve.

Per portion Energy 444kcal/1841kJ; Protein 2.7g;
Carbohydrate 23.8g, of which sugars 23.7g; Fat
38.2g, of which saturates 22.5g; Cholesterol 91mg;
Calcium 65mg; Fibre 1.2g; Sodium 21mg.

Belgian chocolate mousse
Chocolademousse/Mousse au chocolat

Belgium is world-famous for the quality of its chocolate, and Belgians take chocolate consumption very seriously, savouring it in all its forms, from chocolate-filled pralines to this delectable mousse. Every family has its favourite recipe for this culinary classic, usually involving a combination of melted chocolate with fresh eggs and cream, butter, coffee and liqueur. Whatever the recipe calls for, the essential ingredient is the chocolate, which must be of excellent quality.

1 Put the chocolate in a heatproof bowl that will fit over a small pan, or in the top of a double boiler. Half fill the pan or double boiler base with water and bring to the boil.

2 Immediately remove from the heat and place the bowl of chocolate on top, making sure it does not touch the water. Leave until melted, stirring occasionally, then scrape into a bowl and leave to cool to room temperature.

3 In a clean bowl, whip the cream with 12g/½oz tbsp of the sugar until it stands in soft peaks. Set aside.

4 In a separate, grease-free, bowl, whisk the egg whites, gradually adding 50g/2oz/ 4 tbsp of the remaining sugar, until stiff.

5 Whisk the egg yolks in a third bowl, gradually adding the last of the sugar, until foamy. Fold the yolks into the chocolate.

6 Using a spatula, fold in the whipped cream and then the egg whites, taking care not to deflate the mixture.

7 Spoon or pipe into ramekins, dessert glasses or chocolate cups and leave to set for at least 4 hours. Serve plain or with any of the suggested decorations.

Variations
• Use a flavoured chocolate, or add 15–30ml/ 1–2 tbsp of rum, Grand Marnier or Tia Maria.
• The mousse can be made without egg yolks, if preferred.

Serves 4

150g/5oz Callebaut callets (semi-sweet bits) or other good-quality Belgian chocolate, cut into small pieces
200ml/7fl oz/scant 1 cup whipping or double (heavy) cream
75g/3oz/6 tbsp caster (superfine) sugar
2 eggs, separated, at room temperature
Chocolate curls or sprinkles, roasted almond slivers, strips of candied orange peel, cocoa powder or extra whipped cream, to decorate (optional)

Cook's tip
The percentage of chocolate solids in the chocolate influences not only the taste but also the texture of the mousse. The higher the percentage of the cocoa the firmer the mousse will become. It is essential to whip the egg whites while slowly adding the sugar or the whites will separate.

Per portion Energy 550kcal/2290kJ; Protein 5.9g; Carbohydrate 44.3g, of which sugars 43.0g; Fat 40.1g, of which saturates 23.8g; Cholesterol 166mg; Calcium 61mg; Fibre 1g; Sodium 50mg.

Classic Belgian chocolate truffles
Chocolade truffels/Truffes au chocolat

Makes 30

250g/9oz Bolgian dark (bittersweet)
    chocolate, such as Callebaut, chopped
150g/5oz/10 tbsp unsalted (sweet) butter,
    diccd and softened
100m/3½fl oz/scant ½ cup double
    (heavy) cream
15–30ml/1–2 tbsp brandy or a liqueur
    of your own choice
15ml/1 tbsp vanilla extract (optional)
100g/3¾oz/7 tbsp sifted unsweetened
    cocoa powder, icing (confectioners')
    sugar, chopped nuts or grated coconut,
    for coating

Variation

Chocolate-coated truffles Have ready a
baking sheet lined with baking parchment,
and a fondue fork or skewer for dipping.
Use good quality dark or bittersweet
chocolate with at least 70 per cent cocoa
solids. For a glossy coating that retains
its shinc, temper the chocolate. Melt
100g/3¾oz/1 cup chopped dark chocolate in
the top of a double boiler over hot water.
When melted, the chocolate will have a
temperature of around 42°C/107°F. Stir
in 15g/½oz/1 tbsp unsalted (sweet) butter
until smooth, then add an additional
50g/2oz/½ cup chopped chocolate. Stir
the chocolate constantly and keep checking
the temperature. When it registers
32°C/90°F, remove from the heat. Tip the
bowl so that the chocolate pools on one
side. Spear a truffle and dip it into the
chocolate, turning until coated. Let the excess
drain off, then put the coated truffle on the
lined baking sheet to set.

Per portion Energy 101kcal/421kJ; Protein 0.6g;
Carbohydrate 6g, of which sugars 5.9g; Fat 8.1g,
of which saturates 5g; Cholesterol 15mg; Calcium
7mg; Fibre 0.2g; Sodium 10mg.

When made with the best dark Belgian chocolate, these sweet truffles are
the ultimate indulgence. A simple ganache – a rich chocolate and cream
mixture – is shaped and then dipped in a variety of coatings, from cocoa to
tempered chocolate. The latter is pure luxury: a melt-in-the-mouth chocolate
encased in a hard shell. Often flavoured with spirits or liqueurs, truffles are
among the most popular treats sold in Belgian chocolate shops, but with a
bit of patience, they are easy to make at home.

1 Melt the chocolate in a heatproof bowl
over just boiled water, or in the top of a
double boiler, stirring until smooth. Stir in
the butter until melted.

2 Pour the cream into a medium pan and
bring it to simmering point. Remove from the
heat and leave to stand for 2 minutes.

3 Pour the cream into the chocolate, stirring
with a wooden spoon until the chocolate is
completely blended. Stir in the brandy or
liqueur, with the vanilla extract, if using.
Cover and refrigerate for at least 4 hours,
stirring frequently, until stiff but still malleable.

4 With a spatula, transfer the mixture to a
glass tray or shallow dish and spread it out
so that it is 3cm/1¼in deep. Cover and put
in the refrigerator for 5 hours or overnight.

5 Line a baking sheet with baking
parchment. Using a teaspoon, scoop up the
chocolate and use a second teaspoon to
transfer the piece to the baking sheet.

6 Continue until all the chocolate has been
shaped. Put the chocolate back in the
refrigerator for 30 minutes.

7 Working quickly, roll each piece of
chocolate into a ball. Place slightly apart on
parchment-lined baking sheets. Cover lightly
with clear film (plastic wrap) and return to
the refrigerator to firm up again for 1 hour.

8 To coat the truffles, drop them into
separate bowls of cocoa powder, icing
(confectioners') sugar, chopped nuts or
grated coconut until coated. Shake off the
excess coating, reshape the truffles into
balls and lay them on a tray lined with
baking parchment.

9 When all the truffles have been coated,
cover with clear film (plastic wrap) and put
in the refrigerator for 10 minutes to firm up.

10 Store the truffles in an airtight container
in a cool place for up to a week. Serve at
room temperature.

Egg liqueur
Advocaat/Avocat

Advocaat is a liqueur from the province of Limburg, bordering the Netherlands, where the drink is also made. There are two varieties: "thick advocaat", which is solid enough to be eaten with a spoon, and a more liquid version that contains egg whites and is used to make cocktails like the Snowball – a mixture of advocaat, lemonade and sometimes lime juice.

1 Put the egg yolks, sugar and nutmeg, if using, in a very large bowl. Mix gently to combine thoroughly.

2 Stir in the vanilla extract or vanilla sugar, sweetened condensed milk and alcohol.

3 Blend in batches in a blender or food processor for 30 seconds to mix well.

4 Pour into clean bottles, cork and place in the refrigerator.

5 Leave the advocaat unopened for 2 weeks, or longer if you like, so that the flavours mellow and infuse.

6 Shake the bottle occasionally. The colour will intensify as the liqueur ages, eventually becoming the familiar pale yellow of the commercial liqueur.

7 Keep advocaat in the refrigerator and serve in shot glasses, use to make liqueur coffee or pour over ice cream.

Makes 2 litres/3½ pints/8 cups

10 egg yolks
250g/9oz/1¼ cups sugar
pinch of grated nutmeg (optional)
5ml/1 tsp vanilla extract or 8g/⅓oz sachet vanilla sugar
397g/14oz can sweetened condensed milk
1 litre/1¾ pints/4 cups grain alcohol, brandy or good vodka

Cook's tip
Advocaat can be used as an ice cream topping or to flavour desserts and can be stirred into coffee for an indulgent after-dinner treat.

Per portion Energy 5137kcal/21498kJ; Protein 64g; Carbohydrate 481.6g, of which sugars 481.6g; Fat 95g, of which saturates 40.7g; Cholesterol 2159mg; Calcium 1518mg; Fibre 0g; Sodium 661mg.

Makes 1.5 litres/2½ pints/6¼ cups

1kg/2¼lb/9 cups blackcurrants
500g/1¼lb/2½ cups sugar
1 organic unwaxed lemon, sliced
1 litre/1¾ pints/4 cups eau de vie,
    vodka or other clear alcohol
    (95 per cent proof)
1 bottle white fruity wine, about
    750ml/1¼pints/3 cups

Cook's tips
• This recipe can be made with thawed,
frozen blackcurrants or fresh blackcurrants
that are slightly past their best.
• Serve topped with chilled soda water
for a refreshing summer drink.

Per portion Energy 3930kcal/16485kJ; Protein 0g;
Carbohydrate 492g, of which sugars 492g; Fat 0g,
of which saturates 0g; Cholesterol 0mg; Calcium
75mg; Fibre 0g; Sodium 180mg.

Blackcurrant liqueur
Zwarte bessen likeur/Liqueur de cassis

Blackcurrants grow very well in Belgium, and are used in a range of foods,
including jellies, jams, juices, beers and sauces, as well as this delicious
liqueur made with eau de vie or vodka. The liqueur can be mixed with a
fruity white wine, as here, or for a really decadent cocktail, combine it
with champagne to make a Kir Royale.

1 Rinse the blackcurrants until clean, drain
and dry with a clean dish towel. Remove
the stems.

2 Spoon a layer of the blackcurrants into
a large jar. Add a sprinkling of sugar and a
slice or two of lemon.

3 Repeat the layers until all the ingredients
have been used, then stir gently to
distribute the sugar evenly.

4 Cover tightly and leave for 3 days to allow
the sugar to dissolve.

5 Pour the eau de vie or vodka over the
blackcurrants in the jar, replace the lid and
leave for at least 3 weeks or up to 3 months
in a cool, dark place. Shake occasionally.

6 Strain through a fine sieve (strainer)
placed over a bowl, pressing the berries
with the back of a large spoon to extract
as much liquid as possible. Pour into a clean
bottle, cork and store in a cool place.

7 To serve as an aperitif, quarter fill a
champagne or wine glass with liqueur
and top up with chilled white wine.

Coffee with *genever*, Hasselt-style
Hasseltse koffie/Café Hasseloise

Hasselt, the capital of Limburg, is famous for its *genever*. This drink is distilled from a malted grain mash and flavoured with berries from the juniper plant. It is usually drunk neat and very cold, or, as in this speciality from Hasselt, mixed with coffee and topped with whipped cream and chocolate powder or curls.

Serves 1

100ml/3½fl oz/scant ½ cup double
   (heavy) cream
15ml/1 tbsp icing (confectioners') sugar
½ to 1 shot glass (25–45ml/1½–3 tbsp)
   Hasselt Genever
1 shot glass (45ml/3 tbsp) crème de
   cacao liqueur
250ml/8fl oz/1 cup freshly brewed coffee
2.5ml/½ tsp unsweetened cocoa powder
   or 5ml/1 tsp shaved chocolate curls,
   to decorate

Per portion Energy 698kcal/2879kJ; Protein 1.6g; Carbohydrate 12g, of which sugars 12g; Fat 60.7g, of which saturates 33.4g; Cholesterol 137mg; Calcium 57mg; Fibre 0g; Sodium 62mg.

1 Pour the cream into a bowl. Add the sugar and whip by hand or with an electric mixer until stiff.

2 Warm a tall or wide heat-resistant glass, either by filling it with boiling water and letting it stand for 1 minute before draining and drying, or by half filling it with water, heating it on High in a microwave for 30 seconds, then draining and drying it.

3 Add the *genever* and crème de cacao liqueur to the warm glass, then pour in the coffee. Carefully add the whipped cream, letting it slide down the back of a spoon so that it floats on the coffee. Decorate the top with cocoa powder or shaved chocolate.

Diplomat coffee
Diplomaten koffie/Café diplomate

This is a specialty of the Kempen, where a glass of Advocaat often accompanies a cup of coffee. This recipe goes one step further, layering espresso, Advocaat and cream in a tall glass. Creamy and delicious, this is a favourite after-dinner drink, often served with a Belgian chocolate praline.

Serves 1

100ml/3½fl oz/scant ½ cup double
   (heavy) cream
15ml/1 tbsp icing (confectioners') sugar
45ml/3 tbsp Advokaat liqueur
90ml/6 tbsp freshly brewed
   espresso coffee
dusting of unsweetened cocoa powder
   or 5ml/1 tsp shaved chocolate curls,
   to decorate

Per portion Energy 701kcal/2902kJ; Protein 1.7g; Carbohydrate 27.6g, of which sugars 27.6g; Fat 60.7g, of which saturates 33.4g; Cholesterol 137mg; Calcium 65mg; Fibre 0g; Sodium 63mg.

1 Pour the cream into a bowl. Add the icing sugar and whip by hand or with an electric mixer until stiff.

2 Warm a tall or wide heat-resistant glass, either by filling it with boiling water and letting it stand for 1 minute before draining and drying, or by half filling it with water, heating it on High in a microwave for 30 seconds, then draining and drying the glass.

3 Pour the liqueur into the glass. Carefully pour the coffee on top, trying not to disturb the Advocaat layer. Top with the whipped cream, so that it floats on the coffee. Decorate with cocoa or shaved chocolate. Serve immediately.

Liège-style coffee with ice cream
Luikse koffie/Café Liégois

This non-alcoholic coffee and ice cream combination is a speciality of the city of Liège. Enjoy it as an indulgent afternoon treat or serve it after dinner, as the perfect way to finish off a good meal.

1 Pour the cream into a large, grease-free bowl. Sift over the icing sugar and whip the mixture by hand or with an electric mixer, until stiff.

2 Sweeten the espresso to taste by stirring in the sugar.

3 Place the scoops of ice cream in a tall or wide heat-resistant glass.

4 Pour over the espresso and top with the whipped cream. Decorate with a dusting of cocoa, a few shavings of chocolate or the chocolate coffee beans. Serve immediately.

Serves 1

100ml/3½fl oz/scant ½ cup double (heavy) cream
15ml/1 tbsp icing (confectioners') sugar
45ml/3 tbsp freshly brewed espresso coffee
10ml/2 tsp sugar
2 scoops of coffee or mocha ice cream
2.5ml/½ tsp unsweetened cocoa powder, 5ml/1 tsp shaved chocolate curls, or 3 chocolate coffee beans, to decorate

Cook's tip
Chill the espresso before pouring it over the ice cream, if you prefer.

Per portion Energy 925kcal/3855kJ; Protein 6.2g; Carbohydrate 82.9g, of which sugars 81.6g; Fat 64g, of which saturates 40.7g; Cholesterol 166mg; Calcium 198mg; Fibre 0g; Sodium 97mg.

Baking

Bread making in Belgium has been important since medieval times, and the traditions that were introduced by the monks are still evident in the breads on offer today, such as Abbey Bread or soft Belgian Bread Rolls. Cakes, cookies, pies and tarts are also popular, and are often lightly spiced and made with fruit, such as apricots or plums.

Chewy and crumbly

Bread and pastries, pies and tarts, as well as other freshly baked delights, can be found at any bakery, conveniently located in every village or town throughout Belgium. As part of the bread basket of Europe, the tradition of bread baking dates back to when monks made nutritious sourdough-leavened breads in large communal brick ovens using a process of natural leavening known as *Flemish desem*. Traditionally, these multigrain varieties were the staple of a poor Belgian's diet, while the sweeter soft white breads were reserved for the nobility.

Bread remains a key part of the national diet and Belgians love eating it, starting their breakfast, lunch and dinner with different varieties. Stepping into a modern bakery will reveal the overwhelming selection of breads on offer, including numerous choices of healthy grain and seed options as well as delicate white *kramieks* made with milk, eggs and butter. There are also raisin breads, such as the Antwerp speciality *roggeverdommeke*, and the indispensable soft white bread rolls, *pistolets* – an absolute favourite served with butter, fruit jam or chocolate spread on lazy Sunday mornings.

Pies and tarts are well represented in every region, but the province of Limburg is most famously known for its glorious *vlaaien* (pies), based on a yeast-dough crust. These pies are often filled with plums, as in Fresh Plum Tart from Limburg, but can also contain other types of seasonal fruit or a sweet, thick custard. Whatever they contain, any ordinary table displayed with an assortment of *Limburgse vlaaien* is automatically transformed into a modern-day manifestation of Brueghel's famous gluttony paintings.

Cookies and buns are also enjoyed throughout the country, with Brussel's sugar cookies and *mastellen* (cinnamon buns) being among the regional favourites. Lightly spiced, these treats are especially delicious served warm from the oven and are well worth the small effort required to make them at home.

Fresh plum tart from Limburg

Limburgse pruimen vlaai/Tarte au pruneaux de Limbourg

Serves 6–8

250g/9oz/2¼ cups plain (all-purpose)
  flour, plus extra for dusting
50g/2oz/¼ cup sugar
15ml/1 tbsp easy-blend (rapid-rise)
  dried yeast
2.5ml/½ tsp salt
1 egg, beaten
100ml/3½fl oz/scant ½ cup milk
50–75g/2–3oz/4–6 tbsp unsalted (sweet)
  butter, softened

For the filling

675g/1½lb fresh ripe plums, quartered
60ml/4 tbsp soft light brown sugar
15ml/1 tbsp ground cinnamon
15ml/1 tbsp kirsch, rum or sweet
  dessert wine
5ml/1 tsp cornflour (cornstarch)

Cook's tip

To make the pastry in a food processor,
place the flour, sugar, yeast and salt in the
bowl and pulse for 2–3 seconds. With
the motor running, add the egg, milk and
butter. Pulse until the dough forms a ball.
Leave to rise as described in the main recipe.

Per portion Energy 304kcal/1285kJ; Protein 5.9g;
Carbohydrate 57.5g, of which sugars 23.6g; Fat 6.7g,
of which saturates 3.7g; Cholesterol 38mg; Calcium
100mg; Fibre 2.7g; Sodium 56mg.

When natives of Limburg speak of *vlaaien*, they are referring to a type of
tart or pie that is a local speciality. Often depicted by Flemish painters,
vlaaien are made from yeast dough, and can be open-faced, covered or
latticed. Plums are a popular filling, but other types of fruit or even custard
are also used. Traditionally, artisan bakers cook them in wood-fired ovens.

1 Sift the flour into a large mixing bowl. Stir
in the sugar, dried yeast and salt. Make a
well in the centre and pour in the beaten
egg and half the milk.

2 Stir, gradually incorporating the dry
ingredients until the mixture starts to hold
together. Add the extra milk, if needed.
Finally add the softened butter and mix with
your fingertips to a soft dough.

3 On a lightly floured surface, knead the
dough lightly, form it into a ball and place in a
large, lightly oiled bowl. Cover with clear film
(plastic wrap) and leave to rise in a warm,
draught-free place for about 30 minutes or
until doubled in bulk.

4 Meanwhile, prepare the filling. Put the
plums in a bowl. Sprinkle with 45ml/3 tbsp
of the brown sugar and two-thirds of the
cinnamon. Add the kirsch, rum or wine, stir
well and leave to stand while the dough is
rising, stirring occasionally.

5 Preheat the oven to 220°C/425°F/Gas 7
and place a baking sheet inside to heat.

6 Grease a 23cm/9in loose-bottomed tart
or flan tin (pan) and dust it lightly with flour.
Knock back (punch down) the dough. Roll
it out on a lightly floured surface and line
the tart or flan pan without stretching the
dough. Trim and crimp the edges and prick
the base of the pastry case with a fork.
Sprinkle with the remaining brown sugar and
cinnamon. Leave to stand for 15 minutes.

7 Sift the cornflour over the plums, then
layer them in the pastry case. Place the tin
on the hot baking sheet in the oven. Bake for
30–45 minutes or until the pie is cooked and
the pastry is golden brown. Leave to cool on
a wire rack for about 15 minutes.

8 Place the tart or flan tin on a large can.
Using a sharp knife, ease the pastry away
from the sides of the pan. When free, the
sides of the pan will drop down. Lift the pie
off the metal base and put it on a plate.
Serve immediately, in slices.

Variation

Instead of plums, try other fruits such as
apricots, cherries, berries, apples or pears.

Breughel's rice custard tart with apricots
Rijsttaart op zijn Brueghels/Tarte au riz de Breughel

Serves 6–8

250g/9oz/2¼ cups plain (all-purpose)
   flour, plus extra for dusting
50g/2oz/¼ cup sugar
15ml/1 tbsp easy-blend (rapid-rise)
   dried yeast
2.5ml/½ tsp salt
1 egg, beaten
100ml/3½fl oz/scant ½ cup milk
50–75g/2–3oz/4–6 tbsp unsalted (sweet)
   butter, softened

For the filling

500ml/17fl oz/generous 2 cups full cream
   (whole) milk
150g/5oz/⅔ cup short grain rice
50g/2oz/¼ cup caster (superfine) sugar
pinch of salt
5ml/1 tsp vanilla extract
2 eggs, separated, plus 2 yolks
60ml/4 tbsp apricot preserve or
   whole-fruit jam
400g/14oz can apricot halves, drained

Per portion Energy 374kcal/1572kJ; Protein 10.2g;
Carbohydrate 59.3g, of which sugars 20.5g; Fat
11.0g, of which saturates 6g; Cholesterol 145mg;
Calcium 169mg; Fibre 1.4g; Sodium 106mg.

This tart is dedicated to one of the greatest Flemish painters, Pieter Breughel, who is perhaps best known for *De Boerenbruiloft*, a painting that depicts guests at a peasant wedding, tucking into the many different tarts that are such a feature of festive occasions in Belgium. This all-time favourite one, *rijsttaart*, comprises a yeast pastry case filled with sweet apricot preserve and creamy rice custard, and is sold in every Belgian bakery.

1 Sift the flour into a large mixing bowl. Stir in the sugar, dried yeast and salt. Make a well in the centre and pour in the beaten egg and half the milk. Stir, gradually incorporating the surrounding dry ingredients until the mixture starts to hold together. Add the extra milk, if needed. Finally add the softened butter and mix with your fingertips to a soft dough.

2 On a lightly floured surface, knead the mixture lightly, form it into a ball and place in a large, lightly oiled bowl. Cover with clear film (plastic wrap) and leave to rise in a warm, draught-free place for about 30 minutes or until doubled in bulk.

3 Meanwhile, make the filling. Pour the milk into a pan. Bring to the boil, then stir in the rice. Reduce the heat to low, cover the pan and simmer for about 30 minutes, stirring frequently, until all the milk has been absorbed. Stir in the sugar and salt. Remove the pan from the heat and leave to cool.

4 Preheat the oven to 180°C/350°F/Gas 4. Place a baking sheet in the oven. Grease a 23cm/9in springform tin (pan) and dust it with flour. Knock back (punch down) the dough. Roll it out on a lightly floured surface and line the springform pan. Prick the base with a fork.

5 Add the vanilla extract and 1 egg yolk to the cool rice mixture. Stir to mix, then beat in the remaining 3 egg yolks one by one. In a clean bowl, beat the 2 egg whites until stiff, then fold them into the rice custard.

6 Spread a layer of apricot preserve or jam in the bottom of the pastry case. Carefully pour in the rice mixture. Arrange the apricot halves on top, placing them cut-side down. Put the pan on the hot baking sheet in the oven and bake for 35–40 minutes.

7 Place on a wire rack until cool enough to handle, then remove the tart from the pan and put it on a plate. Serve at room temperature with coffee, tea or a sweet dessert wine.

Christmas bread from Wallonia

Waals kerstbrood/Cougnou

Makes 2 small breads or 1 large

250g/9oz/1½ cups raisins

1kg/2¼lb/9 cups unbleached bread flour

50g/2oz/¼ cup sugar

5ml/1 tsp easy-blend (rapid-rise)
   dried yeast

5ml/1 tsp salt

4 eggs, beaten

250ml/8fl oz/1 cup lukewarm milk

250ml/8fl oz/1 cup lukewarm water

250g/9oz/generous 1 cup unsalted
   (sweet) butter, cubed and softened

1 egg mixed with 5ml/1 tsp water,
   to glaze

Cook's tip

The dough can be made in a mixer fitted with a dough hook. Put the dry ingredients in the bowl, add the eggs, milk and water and beat on low speed until the flour is moist. Leave for 5 minutes, raise the speed and gradually work the butter into the dough. Work the dough for 5 minutes more, then add the drained raisins and continue until the dough forms a ball. Remove and knead by hand for 3 more minutes. Proceed as in the recipe.

Per large bread Energy 3278kcal/13799kJ; Protein 67.3g; Carbohydrate 507.9g, of which sugars 126.9g; Fat 123g, of which saturates 70.6g; Cholesterol 654mg; Calcium 1001mg; Fibre 18g; Sodium 1043mg.

This traditional sweet Christmas bread goes by several names, including *cougnou*, *cougnolle* and *coquille*. It is baked in various sizes but always in the shape of the swaddled infant Jesus. When the loaves appear in bakeries at the end of the year, they are often presented as gifts. Butter, eggs and raisins give the breads a cake-like quality, and they are often highly decorated.

1 Put the raisins in a bowl and pour over water to cover. Set aside to plump up.

2 Sift the flour into a large mixing bowl. Stir in the sugar, dried yeast and salt. Make a well in the centre and pour in the beaten eggs and the milk and half the water.

3 Stir, gradually incorporating the dry ingredients and adding more water if necessary, until the mixture holds together. Add the softened butter, a few pieces at a time, and mix with your fingertips until all of it has been incorporated. Knead the dough for 5 minutes. It will be very soft and moist.

4 Drain the raisins and add them to the dough. Knead them in until evenly distributed, then remove from the bowl and knead it on a floured surface for 5–8 minutes more, adding a little more flour if needed. Place in an oiled bowl, cover and leave to rise for 30 minutes.

5 Gently knock back (punch down) the dough, return it to the bowl and replace the cover. Leave to rise for 1 hour at room temperature or overnight in the refrigerator.

6 Divide the dough into 2 equal halves. Leave to rest for 5 minutes, then mould each dough ball into the shape of a baby wrapped in a blanket. To do this, mould the top third into a round for the head, then shape the remainder into an oval, tapering at the base.

7 Place the shaped dough on two baking sheets lined with baking parchment.

8 Brush half the egg-and-water mixture over the loaves, cover and leave to rise for 1 hour or until doubled in bulk. Preheat the oven to 240°C/475°F/Gas 9.

9 Glaze the loaves with the remaining egg mixture. Introduce steam into the oven by spraying it lightly with water from a spray bottle. Bake the loaves for 10 minutes, then reduce the oven temperature to 230°C/425°F/Gas 8 and bake for 20 minutes more until golden.

10 Leave to cool on the baking sheets for about 15 minutes, then transfer to wire racks to cool completely. Serve plain or with butter and jam.

Sugar cookies from Brussels
Grieks brood/Pain à la Grecque

Despite the local name, "Greek bread", this speciality has nothing to do with Greece and is more of an extra-large cookie than a bread. Instead, it got its name from a Brussels' street called *Wolvengracht*, where Augustine monks distributed bread to the poor. From there the bread was dubbed "de Gracht" (bread from the ditch) or "Grecht" in Brussels' dialect. During the French occupation, this was translated as "pain a la Grecque", hence the confusion.

1 Sift the flour into a large mixing bowl. Stir in the sugar, dried yeast, salt and cinnamon. Make a well in the centre and pour in the milk and beaten eggs. Stir, gradually incorporating the surrounding dry ingredients until the mixture holds together.

2 Add the softened butter, a few pieces at a time, and mix with your fingertips until all of it has been incorporated.

3 Shape the dough into a round and knead on a lightly floured surface for 10 minutes, until smooth. Place it in an oiled bowl, cover with clear film (plastic wrap) and leave to rest in the refrigerator for 1 hour.

4 Divide the dough in 5 pieces of equal size and roll each piece into a long roll. Using the palm of your hand or a rolling pin, flatten each roll to a rectangle.

5 Sprinkle the demerara or Turbinado sugar on a plate. Press each piece of dough in turn in the sugar until coated all over. Place on a baking sheet lined with baking parchment and leave to rest for 20–30 minutes.

6 Preheat the oven to 190°C/375°F/Gas 5. Bake the cookies for 20 minutes or until golden. Transfer to a wire rack. The cookies will harden as they cool. Serve as an afternoon snack with coffee or tea.

Makes 5

250g/9oz/5 cups plain (all-purpose) flour
100g/3¾ oz/generous ½ cup sugar
6ml/1¼ tsp easy-blend (rapid-rise)
   dried yeast
pinch of salt
5ml/1 tsp ground cinnamon
30ml/2 tbsp full cream (whole) milk
2 eggs, beaten
100g/3¾oz/scant ½ cup unsalted (sweet)
   butter, cubed and softened
demerara (raw) sugar or organic
   Turbinado sugar, for coating

Cook's tip
The cookies will keep for up to 1 week in an airtight container.

Per portion Energy 430kcal/1807kJ; Protein 7.6g; Carbohydrate 60.2g, of which sugars 22.1g; Fat 19.4g, of which saturates 11.2g; Cholesterol 119mg; Calcium 103mg; Fibre 1.6g; Sodium 154mg

Makes 6–8

500g/1¼lb/5 cups bread flour,
  plus extra for dusting
2.5ml/½ tsp sugar
6ml/1¼ tsp easy-blend (rapid-rise)
  dried yeast
5ml/1 tsp salt
300ml/½ pint/1¼ cups lukewarm water
10ml/2 tsp vegetable oil or softened butter
poppy, sunflower, flax or sesame seeds
  for topping (optional)
butter, honey, homemade jam or Belgian
  Chocolate Spread (see page 21), to serve

Cook's tip

The amount of water will vary, depending
on the absorbency of the flour and the
type of bread required. The dough for
these rolls may be a little wet and sticky,
but this makes the rolls moist.

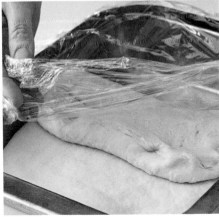

Per portion Energy 239kcal/1013kJ; Protein 5.9g;
Carbohydrate 48.9g, of which sugars 1.3g; Fat 3.6g,
of which saturates 0.5g; Cholesterol 0mg; Calcium
88mg; Fibre 1.9g; Sodium 2mg.

Belgian bread rolls
Pistoleetjes/Pistolets

These bread rolls are a favourite Sunday morning treat in Belgium. People
often order them in advance from their local baker, along with other
breakfast treats like *koffie koeken* (coffee pastries) and sweet or fruited
breads, and carry them home, still warm, to their waiting families. It is
even more rewarding to bake the *pistoleetjes* yourself, however, as they
will infuse the house with the intoxicating aroma of newly baked bread.

1 Sift the flour into a large mixing bowl.
Stir in the sugar, dried yeast and salt. Make
a well in the centre and pour in the water.
Stir, gradually incorporating the surrounding
dry ingredients until the mixture holds
together. Add the oil or softened butter,
a few pieces at a time, and mix with your
fingertips until it has been incorporated.
Knead for 5–10 minutes.

2 Transfer the dough to an oiled roasting
tin (pan) or similar container. Fold it like a
blanket, cover with clear film (plastic wrap)
and leave it to rest in the refrigerator overnight.

3 Divide the dough in 6 or 8 pieces and
shape each into a ball. At this point the rolls
can be coated by rolling them in a damp
towel, then dipping into the chosen seeds.

4 Leaving room for expansion, place the rolls
on a large baking sheet lined with baking
parchment. Using an oiled skewer, make an
indent in the centre of each roll.

5 Cover with a clean dish towel and leave
the rolls to rise at room temperature for
30 minutes or until doubled in bulk.

6 Preheat the oven to 220°C/425°F/Gas 7.
Introduce steam into the oven by spraying
it lightly with water from a spray bottle. Put
the baking sheets in the oven and spray
briefly with water once more.

7 Bake the rolls for 15 minutes or until the
tops are golden brown and the base of each
roll sounds hollow when tapped. Cool on a
wire rack.

Abbey bread
Abdijbrood/Pain d'Abbaye

Makes 2 loaves

75g/3oz/½ cup linseeds, plus water
   for soaking
250g/9oz/2¼ cups strong white bread flour
250g/9oz/2¼ cups wholemeal
   (whole-wheat) flour
250g/9oz/2¼ cups rye flour
15ml/1 tbsp salt
15ml/1 tbsp easy-blend (rapid-rise)
   dried yeast
300ml/½ pint/1¼ cups lukewarm water

For the poolish

75g/3oz/⅔ cup strong white bread flour
75g/3oz/⅔ cup rye flour
2.5ml/½ tsp easy-blend (rapid-rise)
   dried yeast
150ml/¼ pint/⅔ cup water

Cook's tips

• Poolish is a pre-fermentation method,
which gives bread a richer and more
complex flavour, and enhances shelf life.
• Linseeds, which are also sold as flax seeds,
give the bread a nutty flavour and are a
good source of omega 3 fatty acids. Soaking
them makes them easier to digest.

Per portion Energy 1711kcal/7251kJ; Protein
52.1g; Carbohydrate 328.9g, of which sugars 5.2g;
Fat 29.9g, of which saturates 4.3g; Cholesterol 0mg;
Calcium 579mg; Fibre 38.3g; Sodium 1001mg.

In medieval times, abbeys and convents baked every day and distributed
bread to the poor and the sick. Many abbeys still make breads, as well as
beer and cheeses, according to artisan methods. Until the 19th century,
only rye flour was available in Belgium and all bread was therefore "black".
When cheap wheat arrived from America, paler bread was preferred.
A combination of the two produced this nutritious multigrain loaf, which has
become very popular. Start making it the day before baking.

1 Start by making the poolish. Mix all the dry
ingredients in a bowl. With a fork, stir
in the water to make a smooth paste. Cover
the bowl and leave the mixture to stand for
8–12 hours at room temperature.

2 Put the linseeds in a bowl and pour over
120ml/4fl oz/½ cup hot water. Leave to stand
for at least 1 hour.

3 Put the flours into a mixing bowl. Add the
salt and yeast. Make a well in the centre and
add the poolish, with the lukewarm water.
Mix, gradually incorporating the surrounding
flour mixture, until the mixture comes
together to form a dough. Transfer to a lightly
floured surface and knead the dough for
10 minutes.

4 Drain any free water from the linseeds,
then knead them into the dough until well
distributed. Continue to knead for about
2 minutes more. Transfer the dough to an
oiled roasting tin (pan) or similar flat container.

5 Pat it out, then fold it over like a blanket,
cover with clear film (plastic wrap) and leave
to rise in a dry place until it doubles in
volume, about 1 hour.

6 With your fist, knock back (punch down)
the dough, then divide it into 2 equal pieces.
Shape each into a ball or a loaf shape and
place in bread tins (pans) or, for a decorative
appearance, in coiled proofing baskets.
Cover and leave to rise for 30–60 minutes,
until the loaves have doubled in bulk.

7 Preheat the oven to 230°C/450°F/Gas 8.
Introduce steam into the oven by spraying it
lightly with water from a spray bottle. Remove
the breads from the tins or baskets, score
with a knife and transfer to a baking sheet
lined with baking parchment. Put them in
the oven and spray again with water.

8 Bake for 40 minutes or until the loaves
are golden brown and sound hollow when
tapped on the base. Cool on wire racks.

Index

Author's acknowledgements

This book is dedicated to my loving mother and grandmothers who were the inspiration and foundation of my Belgian culinary roots and to my country, which nurtured me with its gastronomic heritage.

My daughters Tine and Lore, may you always keep the best of these traditions alive wherever you may settle, as those loving memories will always bind us.

To Mark, my husband, my greatest support in the kitchen and even more, for his testing, grading and always appreciating the foods I have concocted over the years.

And to Chef Toussaint, who believed in me and directed my culinary passion into a profession, and my many students who inspire me everyday.

Publisher's acknowledgements

The publishers would like to thank the following for permission to reproduce their images (t=top, b=bottom, l=left, r=right): **Alamy** 6bl (Tibor Bognar), 6br (David Noble Photography), 8 (Andrew Critchell), 9tl (Helene Rogers), 9tr (Stephen Roberts Photography), 10b (Visual Arts Library (London)), 11tl (Bildarchiv Monheim GmbH), 11br (Joern Sackermann), 12bl (Stephen Roberts Photography), 12tr (Picture Contact), 13tr (Peter Horree), 13cr (Cephas Picture Library), 15tr (Peter Titmuss); **Corbis** 10tl (Francis G. Mayer), 17tr (Ariel Skelley); **iStockphoto** 7t (Stan Rippel), 15bl (Nathan Wajsman); **Rex Features** 16bl (Ilpo Musto); **Suzanne Vandyck** 13b, 14b, 16br, 17b.